SHALL I RENEW
MY BAPTISMAL PROMISES
NEXT EASTER?

First published in 2012 by
by New Life Publishing, Luton,
Bedfordshire LU4 9HG

©Ambrose Walsh

British Library Cataloguing in Publication Data
A catalogue record for this book is available
from the British Library

ISBN 978 1 903623 63 3

All rights reserved. No part of this book
may be reproduced, stored in a retrieval system,
or transmitted by any means – electronic, mechanical,
photocopying, recording or otherwise without the
prior written permission of the publishers.

Biblical texts from the New American Bible,
Devore & Sons Inc., Wichita, Kansas, 67201. Used with permission. The Acts of Worship: some of the prayers are taken from the Rite of Christian Initiation of Adults 1985 ICEL, Geoffrey Chapman, London, 1987 (composed for use with Catechumens, they are here adapted for use by persons who have already received Christian Initiation).

Typesetting by New Life Publishing,
Luton, UK  www.goodnewsbooks.net
Printed and bound in Great Britain

# SHALL I RENEW MY BAPTISMAL PROMISES NEXT EASTER?

Ambrose Walsh

New Life Publishing

*for Agnes
and the Easter '92 group
who have borne an enduring witness
to the value of this exercise*


*and with thanks to the editorial skills
of Rita Daughton and Brenda Slaughter
and the encouraging support of Kate Duffin*

# CONTENTS

Introduction:   Why Ask the Question? ............................ 1

Chapter One:   A Sense of The Mystery ............................ 17

Chapter Two:   Called and Chosen ...................... 39

Chapter Three: Purified ........................................ 67

Chapter Four:   Enlightened ............................................. 113

Chapter Five:   Entrusted with God's Gifts ..................... 137

Chapter Six:   Initiated into Christ's Church ............... 179

Chapter Seven: A Church with a Sense of Mission ........ 213

Notes: ................................................................................ 225

# INTRODUCTION

# WHY ASK THE QUESTION?

Members of the world-wide communion of Roman Catholics are being summoned to make the Twenty-first Century an age of what is called, 'a new evangelisation.' If we are to answer the call there are various questions we must ask. Some are appropriate for members of the Church wherever it exists; some are particular to the Roman Catholic Church as it exists in our own country.

The questions for all Catholic Christians concern the nature of evangelisation and what is needed in those who are to carry out the task. This book offers for all who wish to answer this call, reflections on what it means to be committed to the life and mission of Christ's Church. Some matters for the consideration of Catholics in England and Wales are offered in Chapter Seven. They concern the way the Roman Catholic Church there has traditionally seen itself and its role vis a vis the rest of British society.

We shall become an evangelising church when we become convinced that the primary task of Christ's Church is to manifest to all and sundry that God invites everyone to share his glorious gift of life in Christ, revealed in the Gospel and shared in the Sacraments of Faith. We shall become an evangelising church when we become convinced that everyone who has responded to the Gospel and been initiated in the Sacraments of Faith has been called to and has been equipped by God's gifts to share in the Church's mission. We shall become evangelists when we become convinced that each of us must be as dedicated to this calling as Catechumens are expected to be when they make their Baptismal Promises. This being so, we can begin our formation as evangelists when we realise that every year, as an integral part of the most solemn act of worship in the year, the Easter Vigil, we are recalled to precisely this re-dedication.

## A FUNDAMENTAL QUESTION

The question "Shall I renew my baptismal promises next Easter?" is meant to stop us in our tracks so that we shall not drift unthinkingly towards a familiar ritual with no expectation that it will make any difference in our lives. There are those, thanks be to God, who, at this moment, will be asking themselves, "Shall I apply for Baptism next Easter?" If we approach our question with the same seriousness as the Catechumens must ask theirs, we may discover that each year in the Church's Easter Liturgy we have been offered a wonderful grace we have not yet averted to.

Consider the matter from the point of view of the Catechumens and their catechists. After a long training, perhaps years, perhaps months, those responsible for the Catechumens' Christian formation must discern whether their charges are ready for Christian Initiation. A number of considerations must be taken into account in making this delicate assessment but the basic requirement must be this: is this person ready and able to make a personal, life-long commitment to the Lord Jesus Christ and his mission. Those discerned to be ready to take this step are invited to prepare for a momentous event. The preparation is a forty day period of what The Rite of Christian Initiation of Adults (R.C.I.A.) calls, "purification and enlightenment."

On Ash Wednesday, the Faithful, that is to say, all who are already baptised members of the Church are invited to do the same. We can begin to be formed as evangelists when we whole-heartedly seek to be renewed in all that it means to be a Christian, empowered by the Sacraments to share the life and mission of Christ's Church. We shall become evangelists if and when we experience the reality of the life-changing grace that Catechumens are taught to look forward to in their Christian Initiation.

I have heard it said by adults who are beginning to realise what it is to have been baptised, "It must be wonderful for this to happen when you are an adult. I see the newly baptised on Easter Night and I think I have missed out on something." Well, it is true that they have missed out on something but it is not because they were baptised in infancy. What they have missed is the formation that is required of all adult converts before baptism but appears not to have been required or may be not even have been offered to those baptised in infancy. In the now widely quoted words of the late Cardinal Suenens, written in

1975, "Catholics these days are being sacramentalised but not evangelized."[1] Well, all is not lost for, if we take seriously the 'purification' that is offered us in Lent, we may confidently look forward to the 'enlightenment' that is promised. This enlightenment will reveal to us not only the wonder of the grace into which we have been called, it will awaken in us a zeal for the mission on which we have been sent.

It may well be that there is in the Church a widespread appreciation of what God can do for individuals and communities who wholeheartedly prepare to renew Baptismal Promises at the heart of the Easter festival. I am not persuaded that there is. My own conversion on this point took some time and it was only when, for years, I had been a pastor of others that I began to realise what I had been missing.

Ordained a priest in 1966, I became a parish priest in 1974. At some time during the seven years I was in my first parish, it dawned on me we were missing the point of Easter. We had developed a very full and widely shared Liturgy of the Easter Triduum. From the Mass of the Lord's Supper until Vespers of Easter Day we did everything, including singing almost the entire Liturgy of the Hours. In those days, for a lot of lay-people, the Church's daily prayer was still something to be discovered and I remember particularly how great a revelation to so many people was the beauty of the Liturgy of Holy Saturday. I have an abiding memory of a young boy, eight or nine, singing with his parents, "Blessed be the Lord, the God of Israel." We loved it.

Looking back I have come to realise that the need for individuals and communities to take seriously the renewal of baptismal promises must have existed seminally in my mind at the time. We advertised the services of the Easter Triduum in the form of an invitation from the Lord to renew the Covenant established in Christ's Death and Resurrection. I recall one touching effect of this practice. A parishioner who carried some serious burdens told me that she was pushing her vacuum-cleaner around, feeling pretty depressed, when she caught sight of her invitation on the mantelpiece and her spirits were lifted immediately. Despite the great joy these celebrations brought us, something was gnawing within me. One year it struck me like a blow: however beautiful our worship, we had failed in our mission. Our community had not brought a single new believer to the Easter Sacraments.

In 1972, the Congregation for Divine Worship had published the Latin text of a new Rite of Christian Initiation of Adults. This had been done in accordance with the decree of the Second Vatican Council, (1962-65) that the Catechumenate be restored. An English translation of this rite would not be available for use in parishes until 1987 but during the nineteen-seventies, I had access to a study edition of the document. I was filled with admiration for the vision of the evangelising Church it described but it seemed too idealistic. Where was the parish community with the vision capable of putting it into practice? With the profoundest respect for the piety and religious observance of individual believers and the parish communities with which I was familiar, I knew no parish that had developed a sense of mission such as the R.C.I.A. expected of those who were to use it. Something was wrong. Something was lacking.

It occurred to me that we could never bring others to make a life commitment to the Lord Jesus, if we continued to treat so lightly the invitation to renew our own – whether as individual believers or as a community with a mission. Years later when a 'Decade of Evangelisation' was announced in preparation for the Third Millennium of the Christian era I felt that it was being radically misunderstood. I heard it preached as something being offered to the 'lapsed' or to a world beyond the Church. Did not our own communities of faith need a 'new evangelisation' if we were ever to evangelise others. It was being assumed, however innocently, that because we are Christ's Church we are automatically equipped for the task. It is important to stress what I call the 'innocence' of this assumption for unawareness creates a much greater blind spot than a deliberate rejection of or indifference to a perceived duty!

Any task needs thinking out: what is our goal, what means do we need to achieve it, do we have these means at our disposal, what must we do to obtain the means we lack? Where the task belongs to each but is common to all, there needs to be discussion, agreements, allocation of resources and responsibilities. Once we have begun the task, there needs to be an on-going assessment of how the plan is working out. So, where do we begin? Shall we start with a parish committee, a diocesan commission, a plan of action and allocation of funds? This would be fine and necessary in any human endeavour.

However, evangelisation, while it requires human effort and the application of our human gifts is, of its nature, a more than human endeavour. It is a work of grace.

To be able to evangelise, whatever the concrete steps that must be taken in terms of planning and resources, is the work of God's grace. To bring people to the Gospel of Christ is the work of God's grace in its origin, in its goal and in the means for its accomplishing. To become an evangelist or to become an evangelising community we need to build on the spiritual foundations that make the work of evangelising possible. What are these spiritual foundations and to what extent are we consciously in touch with them? To what extent do we consciously rely on them?

We are members of a church which claims to possess all those gifts of the Spirit which give structure to the visible Body of Christ on earth: the Sacred Scriptures, the apostolic tradition, the apostolic communion of leadership, the Sacraments. These we call the 'hierarchical' or 'structural' gifts as distinct from the 'free' or 'charismatic' gifts of the Spirit. The Roman Catholic Church has always claimed that it possesses all the hierarchical gifts, identifying it as the visible manifestation of Christ's Church. But does the simple possession of these gifts assure a fruitful exercise of the apostolic mission? If numbers are judged as a measure of success the sharp decline in Mass attendance in the West is enough tell us otherwise.

These are chastening thoughts. What will happen if we permit such questioning to break through assumptions about how well equipped we are for the work of evangelisation? What must we do if, with humility of heart, we allow the awful words of Cardinal Suenens to dawn on us? We may have been introduced to the Sacraments but it may dawn on us that the Lord is calling all of us, clergy no less than laity, to be newly evangelised that we may be made capable of bringing this saving gift to others.

The source of power needed to evangelise is not to be found in human abilities and human gifts, however indispensable these may be in the process. The power to evangelise must be found in Christ's outpouring of the Spirit. It has been said that there can be no mission without a Pentecost. However, the Spirit is Sovereign and manifests his gifts as and where he will. He is in no way constricted by what we call his structural or hierarchic gifts. Indeed, his charisms are essential for the task of evangelising.[2] Even so, it is a fundamental tenet of Catholic Faith that the Spirit is manifested and outpoured in and through the hierarchical or institutional gifts. This is supremely the case in the Sacred Liturgy "the summit toward which the activity of the Church is directed (and) the fount from which all her power flows."[3] One way of recovering the power needed to become an evangelising church is to rediscover and return to this source. In fact, there is a particular need for Catholic Christians to make this rediscovery.

For some Christians the work of evangelising is completed when individuals become listeners to the Word and begin to live a personal life of faith in the living Lord Jesus. For Catholic

Christians the Good News leads beyond this individual act of faith to recognition of the concrete, corporate reality which embodies the Lord's visible presence on earth. Our Catechumens are certainly taught to become listeners to the Word, but the faith thus engendered must lead to a sharing, by sacramental participation, in the mysterious reality acknowledged in the ancient Creeds: Christ's Church. The purpose of the Catechumenate is to express and facilitate the journey from the beginnings of faith in Christ to sacramental incorporation into his Mystical Body. That is why the Second Vatican Council said it must be restored.

If we are to become God's instrument for a manifestation of his grace in a new age of evangelising, we must awaken to what we may have lost consciousness of or which lies only on the periphery of our consciousness. The Liturgy, the core expression of the Church's sacramental reality, invites all who share in it, to be continually renewed in that gift of God which the Church exists to offer others. This need to be constantly renewed in what we are all about is why we regularly participate in the sacramental reality which is both the source and summit of the Church's activities: our need for renewal lies behind the injunction to share in the Mass every Sunday. This, surely, is why the Second Vatican Council said that the weekly celebration of the Lord's Day is the "original feast",[4] the source from which springs the entire annual cycle of Liturgical seasons. Even so, once a year all that the Mass signifies and effects is celebrated most solemnly over a three day feast. At the heart of this feast is the Easter Vigil and there, the whole Church is invited to be open to God's gift of being renewed in the foundations of its Christian calling and empowerment.

Among the potent teachings contained in the R.C.I.A. is the distinction it makes between having a working knowledge of Catholic doctrine and what it calls a 'sense' of the Mystery of Faith. It says that the Catechumenate exists above all, to bring those preparing for Christian Initiation to a 'profound sense' of the mystery they are to share in.[5] How can we bring others to this point, if we fail to examine our assumption that we already live with this profound sense ourselves! Surely Lent asks of us no less than it asks of Catechumens!

As I pondered the fact that every year Lent recalls the whole Church to its foundations, a foolish thought occurred to me: there is only one kind of Lent! It makes no difference who we are or where we are in the journey of faith. Lent offers all the Faithful, as well as the Catechumens, the opportunity of deeper purification and enlightenment with a view to becoming ever more open to what it means to be baptised. Some of us may be Catechumens, others, half-hearted cradle Catholics; some will be deeply committed Christians with half a lifetime's service of the Lord behind them. Even if our community is one of exemplary virtue that has embraced monastic vows of solemn profession, there is still only one Lent. Some of us may even be faithful and devout believers approaching life's end, virtually knocking on Heaven's gate. Whoever we are, all are offered exactly the same Lenten formation. Each person, taking ashes at the beginning of Lent hears the foundational Gospel call:

"Repent, and believe the Gospel." Lent prepares catechumens for the wonder of their sacramental empowerment to live in Christ and share his mission. It offers all baptised members of the Church the opportunity of making a radically new commitment to the same calling and a new opening to the same empowerment in the Spirit.

## THE NEED FOR EXPECTANT FAITH

Reading these words, people already committed to a life of faith and service in the Church may accept the point and resolve with humbleness of heart and generosity of spirit to do all they can to make a new, heartfelt commitment at Easter. However, there is an essential dimension to this Liturgical, sacramental experience which people need to avert to. It is one thing to approach with a new seriousness the Liturgical act of renewing our Baptismal commitment. It is quite another to realise, with an expectant faith, that if we do commit ourselves anew to our Christian calling, the Lord will undoubtedly renew in us all the gifts he first offered us in our Christian Initiation! It is in the action of the Lord, through a new outpouring of the Promised Gift, first given us in our Christian Initiation, by which we become evangelists and the parish community, a people empowered for mission. If it is true that there can be no mission without Pentecost, we should remember the words of Pope Paul VI who said that we should see in the second sacrament of Christian Initiation, Confirmation, the sign of our sharing the grace of Pentecost.[6] The Gift was promised; nevertheless, those to whom the Gift was promised were told to prepare themselves to receive it.

Catechumens are led to the point where they are ready to make a commitment to Jesus as their Lord and Saviour because He has made promises he will undoubtedly fulfil. The Catechumenate experience, and especially the Lenten experience of purification and enlightenment is intended to bring them to such an openness of heart that they receive all that the coming of the Spirit offers. Are we to believe that, at whatever point we may be on our personal journey of faith, or at whatever point our community of faith has come to in its commitment, the Lord will fail to renew us with his gifts if we wholeheartedly renew our commitment?

We easily overlook opportunities to make a new beginning if we approach them without expectant faith. I look back on my life and recall such moments. One, in particular, is worth reflecting upon in the context of the opportunities offered us in the Liturgy to be renewed in the fundamental grace of Christian calling and empowerment. I am old enough to have been 'ordained' a sub-deacon before the Order was abolished.[7] Being made a sub-deacon was an ancient rite and a significant step in one's progress towards priestly ordination for it was on being made a sub-deacon that one accepted the responsibility of engaging in the Prayer of the Church every day and it was at this point that one made a commitment to the celibate life as a sign of one's service to the Church. The rite was not a sacrament but it was regarded as a very solemn moment. It was what is called a 'sacramental', that is to say, an act of worship carried out in the prayer not of an individual but in the prayer of the whole church: a Liturgical act.

As was the custom, one made a week's retreat before the ordination. During such a week in April, 1965, I made an entry in my journal. Quoting the text of the ordination prayer, I wrote, "Bring to fruit in me those gifts of the Holy Spirit I received in Baptism and Confirmation and for which the bishop will pray on Saturday, (when he says) 'Let the Spirit of wisdom and understanding, the Spirit of counsel and fortitude, the Spirit of knowledge and piety rest upon them and fill them with the Spirit of your fear'." I was preparing to make an adult commitment to my Christian vocation by dedicating my life to the service of the Church. That I might be empowered to do this, the Church was to pray for me that I would be renewed in the gifts once given in the Sacraments of my Christian Initiation.

Thirty years later, when I became familiar with prayer for the grace known as 'Baptism in the Spirit', I realised this was the very prayer that had been made on my behalf when I had been ordained sub-deacon. A liturgical prayer had been made over me, with the laying on of hands. The grace which the Church prayed for in the Liturgy of my sub-diaconate ordination was the grace of being renewed in all that had been given me in the Sacraments of my Christian Initiation. Is this not the grace offered to the whole community of faith and each member of it, in every Easter Liturgy?

When the Church prays in the ordination of deacons, presbyters and bishops, it prays that the Holy Spirit will give an anointing as yet not given. It does the same thing in the Sacraments of Christian Initiation. In the sub-diaconate prayer, it prayed that the candidate may experience a new flourishing of gifts already given. This is exactly what we should expect in the Liturgical rite of Easter Night when the whole community is invited to renew its commitment to the Risen Lord:

"Through the paschal mystery, we have been buried with Christ in baptism so that we may rise with him to a new life. Now that we have completed our Lenten observance, let us renew the promises we made in baptism when we rejected Satan and his works, and promised to serve God faithfully in his holy Catholic Church."[8]

When we do so, the Church makes a simple prayer recalling the momentous grace given in our Christian Initiation:

"God, the all-powerful Father of our Lord Jesus Christ, has given us a new birth by water and the Holy Spirit, and forgiven all our sins. May he also keep us faithful to our Lord Jesus Christ."[9]

Imagine what would happen to an assembly of believers whose 'Amen' to this prayer was a resounding declaration of a truly expectant faith! Would not the place in which they were assembled 'be shaken'?[10]

In celebrating the Sacraments, the efficacy of the prayer is not dependent upon the faith and goodness of the minister. We may say, however, that the effectiveness of prayer for a renewal of gifts once given, whether the prayer is Liturgical or otherwise, depends upon the kind of faith the prayer expresses. This prayer is the prayer of the Church, Head and members, and it is rooted in God's utter fidelity to his promises.

I approached the prayer of my sub-diaconate ordination with a hope rooted in my own good intentions that the rite would do me some good. I did not bring an expectant faith, rooted in the Lords own promises! That is what has to change in us. If the Catechumens showed such a shallow faith, could they possibly be judged ready for Christian Initiation? It is out of the question. Every year, Lent invites each and all of us to approach Easter no less seriously than the Catechumens. 'The Faithful' as we are called, must bring to the act of renewing our baptismal commitment nothing less than the seriousness of mind and, above all, the expectant faith with which the Catechumens must make their baptismal commitment.

The Catechumens have every right to expect their sacramental initiation to bring about a radical transformation in their lives because that is exactly what the Gospel promises. We who were initiated into the Mystery of Faith in our infancy are invited every year thereafter to be renewed in that grace. If we can come to a new realisation of all that he calls us to and make a new, wholehearted, commitment to him will he not respond to our faith with the same generosity that he shows the newly baptised? "What father among you would hand his son a stone when he asks for a fish? How much more will the Father in heaven give the Holy Spirit to those who ask him?"[11]

For Catholic Christians, evangelising is a process that leads, via a period of being only a listener to the Word, to the transforming experience of the Easter Sacraments of Christian Initiation. In the Catholic tradition, now happily restored by the Second Vatican Council, those who have come to believe in Jesus Christ must be prepared to undergo a period of indefinite duration wherein the genuineness of their conversion, their fidelity, their perseverance as disciples and their readiness to be apostles is tested before sacramental initiation can even be considered. Only then are they permitted to enrol for Baptism and begin the Lenten period of purification and enlightenment.

Perhaps we may be permitted to look back on the years we have spent keeping faith with Christ and his Church and tell ourselves we have been through as difficult and as searching a time as any Catechumenate. Maybe the time has come for us to embrace a period of purification and enlightenment that will lead not only to a sincere renewal of our baptismal promises next Easter but a profound renewal of the graces offered us in our Christian Initiation. To welcome the Promised Gift with open, purified hearts will be the first step to our becoming the evangelising Church we are called to be.

# CHAPTER ONE

# A SENSE OF THE MYSTERY

## HAVING A SENSE OF SOMETHING

For Catholic Christians, the Sacred Liturgy is at the heart of our religion. At the heart of the Sacred Liturgy is the Holy Mass and at the heart of the Mass, the one presiding, referring to the action that has taken place at the altar, proclaims to the whole congregation, 'The Mystery of Faith'. We would be making a mistake, however, to imagine the Holy Eucharist as existing somehow in isolation from everything else that makes up the manifestation of God's grace in creation. The expression 'The Mystery of Faith' points to the Eucharist as the most perfect expression of something existing in God's creation, the roots of which extend far beyond the moment in which these words are proclaimed. The Holy Eucharist can only take place because of profound changes which have already been effected by God's grace in those who gather to celebrate it.

Holy Eucharist is the heart of the Sacred Liturgy, described as the summit of the Church's activities and the source of its power. Only by becoming engaged in these activities can we become sharers in the Eucharist. The process of involvement begins before we actually become members of the visible church on earth. In the case of persons baptised in adult life it begins with experiences in which they believe God is calling them to faith in Christ. In the case of those baptised in infancy, it begins with the faith of those who ask that the infants be baptised with the intention of leading them in the ways of faith. No matter how we first became involved in the Mystery of Faith, this book offers reflections on what we have become sharers in through Baptism, Confirmation and Holy Eucharist. It does so in the hope of awakening or rekindling a profound sense of the mystery to which we commit ourselves anew when renewing our Baptismal Promises at Easter. This 'sense' of what is to happen to them is expected of those preparing for adult baptism. Indeed, it is to lead Catechumens to this point that the Catechumenate exists. The Rite of Christian Initiation of Adults, as already mentioned, states this quite explicitly. Their Christian formation must give Catechumens *"not only an appropriate acquaintance with dogmas and precepts but also a profound sense of the mystery of salvation in which they desire to participate"*.[1] What does it mean 'to have a sense' of something and what do we mean by 'the mystery'?

There are those for whom Christianity is an idea or a set of ideas, an ideology, a belief system. Whether they regard themselves as believers or not, they have the notion that Christianity offers a happiness that comes from believing in the system. This is not true of Catholic Christianity.

Catholicism does not invite us to put our faith in a set of ideas, a list of doctrines and moral instructions. It does, of course, invite us to believe certain teachings and goes so far as to say that if we decide that we cannot believe them, we could not call ourselves Catholic Christians. However assent to these doctrines or teachings is not what saves us. Catholic faith is not faith in a set of propositions; Catholic faith is *faith in a person*. That person is Jesus Christ. This is the first thing to be clear about.

The second is that our faith in the person of Jesus is not faith in a dead man however good he may have been and however wonderful his teachings handed down to us. It is faith in the one who has overcome death. It is faith in him who, alone, has changed dying from a dead-end into a veritable Passover into eternal life.

The third thing to remember is that our faith is faith in a living person, *more powerfully present among us* than when he walked the earth two thousand years ago.

Those books we call the Gospels and all the other writings gathered into what we call 'The New Testament', were written to proclaim this faith. Sometime in the last decade of the first century A.D., this faith was expressed in words put on the lips of Jesus to strengthen those facing persecution in his name, "Do not be afraid. I am the first and the last, the one who lives. Once I was dead, but now I am alive forever and ever. I hold the keys to death and the netherworld". [2]

Catholic faith is faith in the Living Lord Jesus, present among us to save us, present among us to bring us into the presence of his Father. We accept his invitation to share his life with the

Father, not just by assenting to his teachings, but by receiving his free gift of God's Holy Spirit. Our faith is in his real presence. What is more, our faith, in the person of Jesus Christ expresses our faith in God. In short our faith is the faith Thomas the Apostle expressed when, contrary to everything he imagined possible, he realised he was in the presence of him whom he had known before his crucifixion, and he said to this human being something he had never realised about him before, 'My Lord and my God.'[3]

To renew our baptismal commitment is not to renew an allegiance to the teachings of a dead man. Our commitment is to this Living Christ who invites our faith as our Lord and Saviour. This is the challenge of Christian faith; we have to make up our mind if we recognise Jesus as Lord, and as effectively present in our own lives as he was for Thomas. Does Jesus invite my faith as he invited the faith of Thomas? Can I make Thomas' words my own? Jesus said, during his life on earth, "No one can come to me unless the Father who sent me draw him".[4] If indeed it was by God's gift that Thomas was able to recognise who Jesus truly is, this faith is a most wonderful gift. If God did not inspire Thomas' act of worship, his words are a terrible blasphemy. If there is no God, of course, they are nonsense. We must choose.

The Gospel according to John says that Jesus answered Thomas' confession of faith with words clearly intended for people like you and me, "You believe because you can see me. Happy are those who have not seen and yet believe". The evangelist goes on to say that it is precisely that we may share the faith of

Thomas that he wrote his Gospel. "Jesus did many other signs in the presence of his disciples that are not written in this book. But these are written that you may believe that Jesus is the Messiah, the Son of God, and that through this belief you may have life in his name".[5] When the R.C.I.A. contrasts *"an appropriate acquaintance with dogmas and precepts"* with *"a profound sense of the mystery of salvation"*, it does so that we may realise the difference between a mental assent to doctrines, and faith in a living person.

## NATURAL HUMAN KNOWLEDGE AND FAITH

To have a mental knowledge of Catholic doctrine is to have some knowledge *about* someone. This abstract knowledge is very different from knowing someone personally. Knowing someone personally, however little we may know him is brought about only through *contact*. One way or another, we *meet*. We meet by *being in their presence*, experiencing their action in our lives. It has been said that we can travel in the same railway carriage with someone from Land's End to John o' Groats, but we can never say we met until the other person is prepared to smile and speak to us. Is it possible to have some 'sense' of God's presence or action in our lives?

In our personal prayer, it may sometimes be granted us to have a sense that we are most certainly in the presence of the One to whom we are praying. But God himself is not the object of our understanding. To an extremely limited extent, our ideas *about* him can be the object of our understanding. But these ideas are not God. As the Catechism of the Catholic Church says, quoting the Fourth Lateran Council, "between Creator and creature no similitude can be expressed without implying an even greater dissimilitude".[6] It also quotes St. Thomas Aquinas. "Concerning God, we cannot grasp what he is, but only what he is not, and how other beings stand in relation to him."[7] However, as believers, we come to God equipped not just with the limited intellectual knowledge that human beings can acquire naturally. We come to God believing that he himself approaches us, inviting our faith. He reveals to our faith his real presence and action in our lives. This is not an abstract knowledge that 'there is a God.' It is Thomas's heartfelt confession to someone present, someone recognised: "My Lord and my God."

But how do we encounter this God who invites our faith? Human persons are essentially 'embodied' and a person to person encounter must be 'embodied'. If we are to have a personal encounter with God in Christ, there has to be a human element and a divine element, material element and a spiritual element. For Catholic Christians, the physical is penetrated by the spiritual. The Spiritual is accessible only in the material. If we think of human beings in terms of body and soul, we must not imagine them to be separate entities; they do not occupy higher and lower realms; their relationship is not like oil floating on water. To speak of body and soul is to speak of two aspects of one reality

By God's grace a person may be granted some apprehension of the divine presence in personal, private prayer. This experience, however, is not peculiar to Christians! One becomes a Christian only by personal contact with Christians, that is to say, people who not only believe in God, but believe that he reveals himself to us in Jesus Christ. Meeting people who believe this, one may be drawn to share their faith. When this happens, the interpersonal contact is discerned as the bearer of God's presence in one's life, inviting faith. The event is, we may say, "a concrete reality penetrated by the Divine Presence". In the language of Catholic Christianity, it is a sacramental reality, a mystery. People may come to faith in God through a multitude of different experiences but to come to faith in the Living Christ, people have to encounter other human beings who already believe in his living presence in their lives. At the most superficial level, this is because Jesus Christ is a historical person. At a deeper level it is because the Living Christ invites faith in and through historical events: the words and actions of those who proclaim him in this world. The trigger for what occurs in the depth of a person's soul when he comes to faith in the Living Christ, is what he sees and hears in his encounters with Christians. Christians, however do not exist in isolation from each other.

To become a Christian believer is to be drawn into a pre-existing group. The source of the group's unity is not the agreement of the members. The group is an 'assembly', it is a 'gathering' a 'congregation' or, more commonly in English, a 'church'. The one who gathers this people together is God, in Christ. He gathers them not only by the preaching of the Good News of

Christ, but by the outpouring of his Holy Spirit. This new creation in God's world is the Mystery of Faith in which we are made sharers through the Sacraments of Christian Initiation. We become sharers in the life and mission of the Church by expressing faith not only in things God has done in the past, but by recognising in faith what he is now doing through his Church gathered in the name and power of Christ.

St. Leo the Great says, "There is no doubt that the Son of God took our human nature into so close a union with himself that the one and the same Christ is present, not only in the first born of all creation but in all his saints as well. The head cannot be separated from the members, nor the members from the head. And so all that the Son of God did and taught for the world's reconciliation is not for us simply a matter of past history. Here and now we experience his power at work among us."[8] St. Paul says that through Christian Initiation, "you have died, and your life is hidden with Christ in God."[9] And in his first letter to Timothy, he says, "Undeniably great is the mystery of devotion"[10] If our minds and hearts are not already filled with awe at what God has called us to share, we must pray for this grace. It is only in this gift that we can make or renew our Baptismal Promises effectively.

## MYSTERY OR SACRAMENT

When speaking of 'sacrament' or 'mysterium': a concrete reality, penetrated by the Divine Presence, we are speaking of what we can see, hear and touch, penetrated by God's own presence among us. Is this not the same language as that used in the First Letter of John? Writing about Jesus of Nazareth, the author said,

> *"Something which has existed since the beginning,*
> *that we have heard*
> *and we have seen with our own eyes;*
> *that we have watched*
> *and touched with our own hands –*
> *the word who is life –*
> *this is our subject."*[11]

The word 'mystery' comes to us from the Greek 'mysterion' via a Latin transliteration, 'mysterium'. We are most familiar with it as describing realities beyond *human understanding*, as for example in the expression, 'The Mystery of the Blessed Trinity'. While there are indeed many things we cannot grasp with our limited powers of reason, the word has a wider use.

Sometimes by 'mystery' we mean something hidden from view, something unknowable to us unless it is disclosed or revealed. This is much nearer the ancient meaning of the word. The Catechism of the Catholic Church has something to say on this point which we do well to remember, "We do not believe in formulae, but in those realties they express, which faith allows us to *touch*."[12] This is a very important word. It makes an appeal to our experience of physical sensation to describe the spiritual intimacy with divine realities that faith should bring about. It is speaking of what R.C.I.A. calls a "sense of the mystery." The Letter to the Hebrews seems to speak about the spiritual intimacy with what lies beyond sensation, when it describes the crucified and risen Christ having entered the celestial Holy of Holies as "an *anchor of the soul*, sure and firm, which reaches into the interior behind the veil."[13]

In ancient Christian usage, the word 'mysteries' was not used to speak about a formulation of ideas or doctrines. For this they used the word 'symbolum' - what we call the 'Creed'. (But even there, as we shall see in Chapter Five, to profess the Creed says a lot more than "I believe *that*.." We make the Christian Creed our own by proclaiming, "I believe *in*..") When speaking of those concrete realities which make present for believers the grace of God confessed verbally in the 'symbolum', the ancients used the word 'mysteries' for what we call 'sacraments'. So in the ancient tradition of the Catholic Church 'mystery' and 'sacrament' had the same meaning. Pope Paul VI spoke in this way in his address to the 2nd Session of the Second Vatican Council on 29th. September, 1963. He said, "The Church is a *mystery,* that is to say a concrete reality penetrated by the Divine Presence". The Council itself used the words 'sacrament' and 'mystery' interchangeably in its Constitution on the Church, (21st November, 1964). The first Chapter is entitled, 'The *Mystery* of the Church' and in its opening sentence it says, "...the Church in Christ is, so to speak, the *sacrament* or sign and instrument of intimate union with God and among mankind" [14]

If the Council's use of the word 'sacrament' seems somewhat

tentative, it is because at the time of the Council, Catholic theology was still dominated by a 19th century revival of medieval theology called Neo-scholasticism. In this tradition, the word 'sacrament' had a severely restricted use: it was used exclusively in reference to those events we know as the Seven Sacraments. This was because theologians had discerned in the traditional understanding of these matters, a particular effectiveness in conferring the grace of God not discerned in other activities. These were said to be, in a unique way, effective 'signs and instruments' of the grace they signified. In this way, the seven sacraments are distinguished from other events called 'sacramentals' e.g. the washing of feet on Maundy Thursday. When the Council used the words 'mystery' and 'sacrament' in a much wider sense, it was reaching back beyond the middle ages, re-capturing the language of the Fathers of the Church in the first six centuries. It quoted, for example, St. Cyprian, the third century North African martyr bishop, who called the Church, "the indivisible sacrament of unity". [15]

Back in the nineteen-sixties when I was tussling with the reintroduction of this word into mainstream Catholic doctrine, I was greatly helped by the English liturgist, Fr. J.D. Chrichton. He reminded us that while, for a lot of people, 'mystery' meant nothing more than some kind of intellectual conundrum, we had, in our Catholic usage, a common expression much more akin to the ancient meaning of 'sacrament' or 'mystery'. He said we are all familiar with the 'mysteries' of the Rosary. When we meditate on the mysteries of the Rosary, we do not approach them as some knotty intellectual problems! We contemplate concrete events in the life of Jesus believing that they embody the grace of God.[16] Realising what Fr Chrichton meant by appealing to something so well-known to me, my eyes were opened to what Pope Paul was saying when speaking of the Church as a "concrete reality penetrated by the Divine Presence". For the first time in my life I had some appreciation of what it meant to speak of 'The Paschal Mystery'.

The word 'mysterion' had been used in the Bible to speak of two realities that come together in the person of Jesus Christ crucified and risen. The first of these realities is God's eternal, hidden, *plan* to bring all mankind to himself. This purpose exists eternally; God's action in this world, revealing and accomplishing it, is something distinct. God's purpose for us may well be written into our innermost being, but it is, nevertheless, hidden from all human wisdom. It is beyond our human grasp. However, God has disclosed or revealed his plan in Jesus Christ, crucified and risen. Here you have the two elements: the eternal, divine reality, and the historical, human realities by which what was hidden is now disclosed; and can be humanly apprehended. For this reason, the word 'mystery' or 'sacrament' was used of Christ himself in the ancient church. The title was resurrected in modern times by the book, 'Christ the Sacrament of Encounter with God'.[17]

The Church Fathers extended the word further to speak about those concrete realities in which we encounter Christ's living presence among us: the Sacred Scriptures and sacramental worship. The immediacy of this powerful presence of Christ in his Church is expressed in the words of St. Augustine, "Peter may baptise but it is He that baptises; Paul may baptise yet it is He that baptises; Judas may baptise, still it is He that baptises".[18] Catholic faith in the effective presence of the Risen Lord which the concrete realities of our regular worship express, is graphically spoken of in the words of St. Leo the Great. This pope, always to be heeded in his descriptions of what the Sacred Liturgy is all about, said that at Christ's ascension, "the visible presence passed over into the mysteries/sacraments."[19]

Ultimately, the word was extended to the totality of the reality which expresses itself in word and sacrament: the Church. St. Augustine, once again: "Let us rejoice then and give thanks that we have become not only Christians, but Christ himself. Do you understand and grasp, brethren, God's grace toward us? Marvel and rejoice: we have become Christ. For if he is the head, we are the members; he and we together are the whole man.... the fullness of Christ then is the head and the members. But what does 'head and members' mean? Christ and the Church."[20] The entire Catholic tradition of faith lies behind the desire of both the Catechumenate and this book that we should awake to a 'profound sense of the Mystery' we have been incorporated into by the Sacraments of Christian Initiation.

The Church knows that we need a lot of Christian formation to appreciate these matters, that is why the Catechumenate can be quite lengthy. Hopefully, we have assented to this formation throughout our lives. The 'adequate acquaintance' with doctrine catechumens are to acquire, is something already given those of us who were baptised in infancy. Indeed, people exposed to what was popularly known as 'the penny catechism' know that they received rather more than an 'adequate acquaintance' with doctrine. This kind of knowledge, however, is nothing more than the appeal to the mind mentioned at the beginning of this chapter. Much more important than this food for the mind, is the Christian formation the Catechumenate provides, for it leads to a radical conversion which exposes us to the heart of Catholic Christianity. We encounter the Divine, revealing himself and accomplishing his purpose in concrete realities: Christ in his Church, acting in our lives principally through its worship in word and sacrament.

## ARRESTED BY THE REALITY OF THE 'MYSTERY'

If it has not already happened there must take place in us something of the life-changing experience of Isaiah. I imagine the Levitical priest, Isaiah, pottering about the Temple in Jerusalem one day, performing the familiar rituals of temple worship when, out of the blue, the same old stuff became a life-changing event. He was given the gift of 'Fear of the Lord' or as we would say in modern English, 'Awe in the Presence of the Lord'. Consider what a life-changing event took place!

Just as we have been familiar all our lives with the sacraments of faith, this man had known the realities of daily Temple worship since his childhood. Suddenly, what was so familiar revealed itself as a concrete reality penetrated by the Divine Presence. "Woe is me, I am doomed! I am a man of unclean lips, living among a people of unclean lips; yet my eyes have seen the King, the Lord of hosts!" [21] In this moment, he realised that he, a priest of the Thrice-Holy God, and all Israel, the people the Holy One had bound to himself in covenant, had no 'sense of the mystery' in which they were involved. If we can share something of the grace given to Isaiah, we shall indeed be renewed in sharing both the life of the Church and its mission. We may begin to prepare for next Easter by reflecting on this grace.

The first Lenten Preface, in the now discarded English text of the Roman Missal, sums up what a well-lived Lent is meant to achieve. About whom do the words speak? Catechumens, as yet only listeners to the Word, are dismissed before the Eucharist is celebrated. These words, then, apply to the Faithful, those who are already baptised and confirmed communicants:

> *"Each year you give us this joyful season*
> *when we prepare to celebrate the paschal mystery*
> *with mind and heart renewed.*
> *You give us a spirit of reverence for you, our Father,*
> *and of willing service to our neighbour.*
> *As we recall the great events that gave us new life*
> *in Christ, you bring the image of your Son to*
> *perfection within us."* [22]

What are these great events? Clearly they refer directly to the

Paschal Mystery, the events of Christ's Passion and Resurrection celebrated with great solemnity in the Easter Triduum. But the mysteries of Christ the Head are also the mysteries of the members of the Body of Christ. May we say then that these words also refer to those great events in our own personal histories which made us sharers in the Paschal Mystery? The sacramental events which gave us new life in Christ are the Sacraments of our Christian Initiation. When we renew our baptismal promises at Easter we recall what a great and wonderful reality we have become a part of. What a vain and empty gesture it would be to 'recall' them in so solemn an act of worship as the Easter Vigil, and to spend forty days preparing to do so, without bringing to their remembrance that seriousness of intent and expectant faith which the Catechumens are to bring to their first Easter Vigil.

Let these be the questions and considerations that guide our preparation to renew Baptismal Promises next Easter: What have we become through Baptism? What have we become involved in? What are the consequences for the rest of our life? God has called us, he is leading us and he will bring to fulfilment the good work he has begun in us.

## POINTS FOR FAITH SHARING

As I look over my past life, what preparation
have I given hitherto for renewing my
baptismal promises at Easter?

We may have learned about the 'character'
that the sacraments of baptism and confirmation
'impress on the soul'. (Cat. Of the Cath. Church. No.1121)
What does it mean to me that I am permanently changed
by my Christian Initiation. Do I think of my baptism as
something in the past rather than something that endures?
"I WAS baptised" as distinct from "I AM baptised."

Do I believe that in making a new and more radical
commitment to God in Jesus Christ, I can be renewed
in all the gifts God wishes me to have through being
baptised, confirmed and admitted to the Eucharist?

## AN ACT OF WORSHIP

## A Hymn

### Opening Prayer:
Father, you have called us together, so that being prayerfully attentive to your holy word, we may prepare ourselves to celebrate worthily all that you have called us to share in Christ, crucified and risen. Awaken in us a new sense of your presence in our lives through the sacramental union you have granted us in our Christian Initiation. We make our prayer etc.

### Old Testament Reading: Isaiah 6.1-9 (Call of Isaiah)

### New Testament Reading: Colossians 1, 12-20
(Praise for our calling into the Body of Christ)

### Gospel: Luke 24, 13-35
(disciples recognising the presence of Christ)

### Intercessions:
The Lord has assured us that whoever asks will receive, whoever searches will find, whoever knocks will have the door opened. Trusting this word we make our prayer:
**Father, grant us a new sense of the Mystery of Faith.**

We come together asking to be renewed in all that it means to be baptised, confirmed and admitted to the Holy Eucharist.
**Father, grant us a new sense of the Mystery of Faith.**

We pray for a new and profound sense of having been called by God.
**Father, grant us a new sense of the Mystery of Faith.**

We seek a new awareness of having been raised from sin to new life in Christ.
**Father, grant us a new sense of the Mystery of Faith.**

We open our hearts to a new outpouring of the Spirit given us in Baptism and Confirmation.
**Father, grant us a new sense of the Mystery of Faith.**

We ask the intercession of Mary, that we may share the grace of responding to God's call as she did: Hail, Mary….

Offering himself on the cross, Jesus entrusted himself into the arms of his Father, let us entrust ourselves now and in the months ahead, praying in the words He gave us:
Our Father…

Father, we praise and thank you for the grace you have granted us throughout our lives even to this day. We thank you for the word and example of others, through whom you called us and set our feet in the way of faith. We thank you for their witness, and pray that you have received them into your heavenly home. We thank you for your faithful love in recalling us, if and when we have departed from our Christian calling, and for the grace by which you sustain us in the pilgrimage of faith. We ask you now to grant us a new and lasting appreciation of all that you have called us to, that we may live as true disciples and apostles of your son, ever ready to share with others your gifts to us. We make our prayer etc.

## A Hymn and a Blessing

*The considerations offered for reflection and prayer
in the following five chapters are based on
acts of worship in which the Faithful
and the Catechumens take part during the
forty days of enlightenment and purification
which is Lent.*

*These acts of worship are*

## The Rite of Election
The First Sunday of Lent

## The Scrutinies
The Second, Third and Fourth Sundays of Lent

## The Presentations
The Fourth and Fifth Weeks of Lent

## The Ephphatha
Holy Saturday

## Christian Initiation into the Paschal Mystery
The Easter Vigil

# CHAPTER TWO

# CALLED AND CHOSEN

*God calls us to faith in Christ; his Church discerning this,
chooses us for Christian Initiation*

## A SENSE OF VOCATION:
## GOD IN CHRIST CALLS ME

Do you recall the story of the boy Samuel? Samuel was brought up from his infancy in the shrine of the God of Israel in Shiloh. He had been dedicated to the service of the Lord by his mother and the scriptures touchingly speak of how she would bring him a 'little tunic' she had made for him when she and her husband visited the shrine each year.[1] The Scriptures describe him as 'ministering to the Lord in the presence of Eli' the high priest. We may say that life in the shrine was his entire life. However, extremely familiar with the Lord's Sanctuary as he was, it is said of the boy, 'Samuel had as yet no knowledge of the Lord and the word of the Lord had not yet been revealed to him.'[2] This part of the story reminds me of my childhood and youth, growing up with a working knowledge of life in the Catholic Church: prayers at home, moral instructions, regular worship in church, a devotional life very much of its time, that is to say the non-liturgical devotions that characterised popular Catholicism in the 1940s and

1950s. It was all very good, all very pious. However, as yet nothing about it spoke to me personally and directly.

God was a long way off, as was only fitting, what with Him being Almighty and me being, well, little old me! I experienced life in the Catholic Church as the recipient of instructions and practices that were there for all, but for no one in particular. God was someone who had revealed himself a long time ago to other people. What had been made known to them had been passed on to my generation. With this information, I was to get on with my life. If I may put it this way, I was quite conscious of what *I* was doing in my religious life but not conscious that *God* was doing something even more real! I was quite ready to go along with the religious expectations of the Catholic culture in which I grew up. Indeed, I was ready to fulfil them because I already had some faith that in living in accordance with these concrete instructions, rules, religious practices and devotions, I was actually obeying the unseen God. But this God was, in a sense, unknown to me, and I saw no reason why he should be bothered to reveal himself to someone as ordinary as me. It is not as if I was the Blessed Virgin Mary or 'St' Peter or 'St' Paul. What had I done, unlike them, to be worthy of being treated like that? The idea simply didn't enter my mind.

To say that, as yet, Samuel had no knowledge of the Lord cannot mean that he was ignorant of things *about* God or ignorant of *things God had done for Israel*. Such knowledge must have been part of his daily life just as the great mysteries of Catholic Faith were part of my daily life. However, as yet, he had no awareness that the God of Israel knew him and cared for him personally. He had no awareness that he had been brought, by God's providence, through the faith of his mother and father, into a situation in which he was being prepared to receive the Lord's personal invitation to become engaged in all that God was doing in, through and for Israel.

Like Samuel, each one of us has to be awakened to the reality that God is personally calling us into the mystery of his dealings with mankind. What God offers all mankind, he is offering me personally. The former reality is no greater than the latter. The first step to renewing our Baptismal Promises has to be a recovery of the first step towards Baptism. That first step is a sense of the reality of our Christian Vocation. Let this be the meditation that this chapter leads to:

**God is no more really present in his universal call to all mankind for the salvation of the whole world than he is in his personal approach to me.**

My personal response to God's call is no less important to him than the response of all mankind. This is what was meant when I was told as a child that had I been the only sinner in the world, God would still have come in the person of Christ, to do for me personally all that the Creed says he did for all mankind.

When we were children we learned that God made us to 'know him, love him and serve him in this life and to be happy with him forever in the next'. As a child I learned these words and it was only to a child's mind that they had any meaning. I was too immature to know what it could possibly mean for one adult to say to another, 'I love you and want to spend my entire life with you.' I was too young to know that the only way I could become the person I was created to be, was to recognise how deeply I was loved. I had to become aware of God's absolute commitment to my well-being, and to realise that it is only by a freely chosen, adult response to so great a calling that I could become all that I had been given life to become.

Let me put it another way. While I knew all the words in which the Christian faith is expressed, words such as 'grace', 'forgiveness', 'holy Communion' etc., my actual religion was more a natural religion, a man made system for dealing with life's imponderables than a personal response to God disclosing himself, and his purpose for me, in Jesus Christ.

I had learned that it was reasonable to believe in a God who had created all things and who, being almighty, deserved my worship and obedience. I fulfilled these duties by obeying his commandments. God had given his orders through Moses but it had been a bit of a waste of time, because people ignored both him and the prophets sent after him to get people to buck up their ideas. In the end, God sent his only son to make sure the message got home, but people did the same to him. I, however, was lucky because I had been brought up with a knowledge of what God wanted of us and now I knew it, I could be confident that if I kept my nose clean and persevered to the end, I would pass muster on the day of judgement. In effect, life was an obstacle course which I could deal with through the knowledge of God's moral law. Religion was essentially morality, and morality meant obedience to the Law of God.

To the extent that any grasp of Catholic Doctrine entered the picture, it formed an impersonal background to my own moral efforts. God had created all things good but man had sinned so God had to start again. He did this in Jesus who died, rose from the dead and ascended into heaven. I learned that Jesus had to die because sin had made such a mess of God's creation. I wasn't exactly sure what the connection was between Jesus dying and God forgiving sin, but at least I could be grateful that he had done so. His rising from the dead and ascending into heaven was nothing to do with me, more a case of his returning from whence he came after having done what he was told to do.

In the nineteen sixties, Karl Rahner shocked a lot of people by observing "Despite their orthodox confession of the Trinity, Christians are, in their practical life, almost mere 'monotheists'. We must be willing to admit that, should the doctrine of the Trinity have to be dropped as false, the major part of religious literature could well remain virtually unchanged."[3] I can see what he meant. Of course I could make the sign of the cross in the name of the Father, and of the Son and of the Holy Spirit, but that there were three persons in one God was nothing to do with me. I had no real appreciation of the fact that by his cross and resurrection Christ had set us free for a personal relationship with God the Three in One. I had no idea that in baptism I had passed with him from death to life and that this life was an outpouring of the Spirit, in which I was adopted and enabled to call God, "Abba". I had no idea that I lived in the Trinity and the Trinity in me. I had no idea that I was a concrete reality penetrated by the Divine Presence.

There was a period in the history of salvation when the point at which The Divine and the human met was thought of as a place: Jerusalem and the Temple which sanctified the city. Profoundly symbolic rituals impressed upon people the utter holiness of God and the privilege of having anything to do with Him. There was the court of the Gentiles at the outermost reaches of the Temple, and a wall which excluded them from inner access. Within, there was the court of the women and within that the court of Israel. Closer to the heart of the complex was the court of the Levites and further in, the Holy Place where the priests carried out the daily sacrifices. At the heart of it all was the Holy of Holies, the 'sanctuary' where nobody entered, except the High Priest and then only once a year. What more impressive symbols can one imagine to teach people the abyss of unworthiness segregating even the chosen people within the mass of humanity from the All Holy?

When we reflect on this, there may begin to dawn on us something of the greatness the Gospel of Christ calls us to in our Christian Initiation. St. Paul, referring to the insurmountable barrier between Israel and the rest of mankind, says of Jesus, crucified and risen, "Remember that at one time you, Gentiles in the flesh... were without hope and without God in the world. But now in Christ Jesus you who once were far off have become near by the blood of Christ. For he is our peace, he who made both one and broke down the dividing wall."[4] In the First Letter of Peter, the writer invites us "Come to him, a living stone, rejected by human beings but chosen and precious in the sight of God, and, like living stones, let yourselves be built into a spiritual house to be a holy priesthood to offer spiritual sacrifices acceptable to God through Jesus Christ."[5]

Jesus spoke of his body as fulfilling all the Jerusalem Temple promised when he said, "Destroy this temple and in three days I will raise it up."[6] and St Paul said, "Do you not know that you are the temple of God, and that the Spirit of God dwells in you?[7] The Jerusalem Bible commenting on its translation 'God's temple' points to the Greek word, *'Naos'* indicating that St. Paul meant the innermost part of the Temple, the 'sanctuary' where God dwells. Each Christian, each member of the Body of Christ is called the 'sanctuary'. Later in the same epistle he says, "Do you not know that your body is a temple of the Holy Spirit within you, whom you have from God and that you are not your own."[8]

In another place, St. Paul says that if Christ is not risen, we are not just foolish we are blasphemers for dishonouring the Living God by associating him with the cross. To his devout contemporaries, to teach that all that Temple worship had symbolised and promised was now fulfilled in the hearts of one-time pagans, must have appeared as the most horrifying blasphemy. How great is our intimacy with God. He has made it possible by raising Jesus from death and calling each and every believer to receive the outpouring of the Spirit in whose power Jesus now lives! Everything about us, all aspects of our humanity, have been taken up to God in the incarnation of his only Son, and this Son, having purified us from all sin through his death and resurrection, has made us sharers in the mystery of mankind's entry into the Holy of Holies. This he has done through the Sacraments of our Christian Initiation, bringing us into and making us living members of that visible, tangible reality which is Christ's Church.

This sign of reconciliation between God and mankind and among men, is no longer a building of stone. It is an assembly of living persons, a communion of persons living in Christ, manifesting this life to the rest of the world by the way they live. No longer servants obeying their master's law for a decent wage, they are sons and daughters, heirs with the Heir, inspired to holiness of life by the very Spirit of God, and drawing others to recognise and embrace the grace in which they stand.

That I, little old me, had been called by God into so great a mystery was obscured for me. As in a 'Chinese' whisper, what I heard was not quite what God, in the living Christ, speaking to me from the heart of his Church was actually saying. However, because this concrete reality, the visible community of faith into which I had been baptised, is indeed penetrated by the Divine Presence, the door was always open for me to be able to step beyond what I thought I already knew. I was able to be conducted by the Spirit into depths I did not know existed. The Way was always open for me to realise that what I had heard had happened a long time ago to one man called Abraham was happening to me: the Living God was calling me into a new way of living, a way of living which I, as yet, knew nothing about, although I thought I knew it all.

When Abraham was called by God to leave his country behind, all that had been true, all that was good in his life up to the moment of his call, was not now discarded as so much rubbish. All had been instrumental in the Lord's preparation for this moment. However, as we see in the life of every person throughout history who has answered God's call, a choice has to be made: do I believe in the presence of the Living God actually calling me in a way I have yet to discover? Do I entrust myself to Him who invites me to find life's meaning in his purpose for me? God has to break into our own little world if we are to become who he created us to be. He calls us to go where we would otherwise never think of going, for the simple reason that we have no idea that such a move is possible. It has not entered into the heart of man to conceive what God has in store for those who love him.

God is calling us to live by faith, faith in the reality of his presence in our lives, faith in the reality of his action in our lives, faith in his eternal interest in our personal well-being.

Certainly this faith involves our assent to matters we could never have known about had they not been revealed by God. But these doctrines are not the object of our faith. The living Lord they describe, the action of this Lord here and now in my own life, is the object of my faith.

When a person discloses to you how much you mean to him or her, when somebody hopes that the pair of you might create a new life together, when someone invites you into a life-long mutual commitment, it is prudent to find out all you can about him or her. This is like getting to know your Catholic Doctrine. However, deciding whether or not you believe in the commitment that is being offered is quite another matter. Your choice to make or not make the commitment is an even more serious matter. Not only the head, but the heart and your entire future life are involved in your response. This is the challenge of God's invitation to us to live by faith. It is not just faith that he exists; it is faith in the reality of his saving action here and now in the life I am living. It is faith that he is calling me into a new relationship with him in Christ.

This is the faith to which God calls us in Christ. This is the faith we declare and celebrate in baptism. It is a faith that God is totally committed to our salvation, as he has revealed in the dying and rising of his Son, Jesus Christ. Our Christian vocation is not just some event in the past. That God calls us is the *enduring foundation* of our life in Christ. The first step towards renewing our Baptismal Promises is to awaken to a renewed sense of being called by God.

## POINTS FOR FAITH SHARING

Have I ever thought of myself as being
called by God as Abraham was?

Do I believe that my response to being
called by God is as important to him as the
response given by the Blessed Virgin Mary
to her calling?

Do I believe that what God calls me to
goes beyond all that he called
even John the Baptist to,
for it is nothing less than life in Christ.

# AN ACT OF WORSHIP

## A Hymn

### Opening Prayer

Father, as we begin our preparation to renew our baptismal promises, we come before you because you have called us. We give thanks that you call us personally and that you call us to come together. We ask your blessing on all we do to answer your call during these days of preparation for Easter. Renew us by your gift that we may proclaim your name to all whose lives we touch. We ask this through Christ our Lord.

### Old Testament Reading: The Call of Samuel, 1 Samuel 3, 1-10

### New Testament Reading: The Call of Lydia, Acts 16, 11-15

### Gospel: The Call of Nathanael, John 1, 43-51

### Intercessions:

We pray to him who knew us before we were born and who through the faith of others has made known to us the Good News of Jesus Christ. We pray in these words:
**Lord, fulfil in us the work you have begun.**

Our being called by God is the enduring foundation of our life in Christ; may the Lord grant us a new awakening to the

privilege to which we are called.
**Lord, fulfil in us the work you have begun.**

The Lord has called us to receive his gifts to all mankind in Christ and to share what we have received with others. May He enable us to fill our calling both as disciples and apostles of the Lord Jesus Christ.
**Lord, fulfil in us the work you have begun.**

There are specific persons whose lives we touch. We pray for them in all their needs. May they find in our faith, hope and love, the Lord's reaching out to them.
**Lord, fulfil in us the work you have begun.**

We commend to the Lord all those who during their lives on earth were for us by their words and example, witnesses to the faith we seek to live by. May they share in the fullness of Christ's redemption.
**Lord, fulfil in us the work you have begun.**

Mary the Mother of the Lord, is our model in answering God's call. We ask her prayers: Hail, Mary….

He who called us has taught us to pray in spirit and in truth, so we say: Our Father..

Father, you have called us from ignorance and darkness into your own wonderful light, revealed in Jesus Christ your beloved son. Grant us a new awareness of our calling to the grace of adoption through the outpouring of the Holy Spirit and be glorified in the witness to your grace that we bring to others. We ask this through Christ our Lord

## A Blessing and a Hymn

# A SENSE OF HAVING BEEN CHOSEN

When a person applies to join the Catechumenate this dialogue takes place:

*"What do you ask of God's Church?"*
*"Faith.".*
*"What does faith offer you?"*
*"Eternal life."*

Before being admitted to the Catechumenate, they are reminded of what God had already done, what he is now doing, and what he will do for them:

*"God gives light to everyone who comes into this world; though unseen, he reveals himself through the works of his hand, so that all people may learn to give thanks to their creator. You have followed God's light and the way of the Gospel now lies open before you. Set your feet firmly on that path and acknowledge the living God who truly speaks to everyone. Walk in the light of Christ and learn to trust in his wisdom. Commit your lives daily to his care so that you may come to believe in him with all your heart. This is the way of faith along which Christ will lead you in love toward eternal life. Are you prepared to begin this journey today under the guidance of Christ?"*[9]

As this admonition spells out, the prospective Catechumens *have already become believers.* They have come to a knowledge of the salvation Jesus Christ offers and they came to this knowledge through their personal contact with faithful Christians. They are now ready for the next step. With their assent, they are admitted to the Catechumenate. They embark upon a long period of instruction and formation in the Christian faith and way of life as it has been handed down to us in the Catholic Tradition. This formation will continue for as long as it takes. It would be supremely foolish to rush it. It must last until both those responsible for their formation, and the candidates themselves, arrive at the point where they believe the time has come to seek Christian Initiation. Catholics baptised in infancy need a conversion of mind and heart on this very point of Catholic Tradition. If a person is responding to the Word with all their heart and mind, it is of no consequence whatever at what point on the journey of faith they have reached. The moment will come, in the fullness of time when they and those responsible for their Christian formation discern that the time is ripe for Christian Initiation.

This process happened the other way around in the lives of most of us who are Catholics today. We began our Christian Initiation on the faith of others, before we could think or choose. We were admitted to Holy Communion and Confirmation before we could make anything more than a child's choice in these matters. However, as time has gone on, sometimes through the ordinary day by day attempts to live as Christians, sometimes through events that challenged our faith to its foundations, we have been so formed that we have come to this day in our pilgrimage of faith. We have come to this point by repeatedly making choices. If we are to prepare ourselves to repeat yet again the great choice which Baptismal Promises represent, it will help us enormously if we can gain some sense that God's choosing us is the very origin of the grace that enables us to choose Him.

Having kept faith with their calling through the long period of the Catechumenate, the time comes for believers to step up for Christian Initiation. They do so in an act of worship which expresses their choice, by writing their names in what is called the Book of the Elect. This is an earthly sign of a heavenly reality: God's choice of them. This rite takes place on the First Sunday of Lent and in signing up, Catechumens undertake to embrace forty days of preparation. This preparation for the Sacraments of Faith is summed up in the words, "purification and enlightenment". The Elect are prepared by prayer and other rites to open their hearts to all that God wants to offer them in Baptism, Confirmation and Holy Eucharist.

Between now and Easter all who read these words can do likewise. If we were baptised in infancy we did not undergo the Lenten rites designed to steer Catechumens towards purification and enlightenment. Reflecting on these rites, making them our own in our prayer, we too may undergo purification and enlightenment with a view to renewing our baptismal promises.

## THE RITE OF ELECTION (First Sunday of Lent)
### *I CHOOSE; THE CHURCH CHOOSES; GOD CHOOSES*

Speaking to a group of young people who had been preparing

for confirmation during the early 1980s, I said to them, "What would you think if when the Archbishop comes next week he said (and here I pointed to different members of the group) 'I have decided that you should be ordained a deacon; you two over there, I shall ordain priests and you, sitting in front of me, I shall give serious thought to ordaining bishop'." Their predictable reaction was one of alarm. A typical reply was, "I would get out of here right away."

I used this shock tactic in an attempt to impress upon them something that I thought they may not have averted to. The fact that they were, at the age of thirteen or fourteen, members of the Confirmation group, meant that they needed no reminding from me that they were there by their own personal decision. They themselves had *chosen* to ask for confirmation. I wanted to impress upon them that while this was undoubtedly true, it was even truer that *God had first chosen them* for this gift. The Church celebrates this belief when a bishop decides to celebrate the sacrament in which the Gift is given.

On the advice of others who have been involved in the preparation of the candidates, the bishop makes a decision, a choice. Just as the candidates made a decision and chose to offer themselves for the sacrament, so the minister of the sacrament makes a choice: he decides to grant them the gift they seek. For him to do this without reference to the will of God would be a great blasphemy. In fact in choosing to worship God by celebrating this sacrament, he directly and clearly affirms the Church's faith that God himself has first chosen the candidates. To do otherwise would be a sin.

In speaking to the Confirmation candidates in the way I did, I was appealing to the high consciousness Catholics have in regard to a vocation to the priesthood. I did this because we have to allow the Spirit to awaken in us an equally clear consciousness of our vocation to the Christian way of life. God's choice of persons to receive an ordained ministry in the Church can have no meaning if it is not more radically, fundamentally true about those who are called to Baptism, Confirmation and Holy Eucharist. The Church celebrates its faith that this is the case in the Rite of Election.

The Bishop summons by name those who have chosen to offer themselves for Christian Initiation. Having listened to the testimony of those who have observed the Catechumens' development and have assisted in their growth, he exercises his own personal judgment and in doing so, exercises also his apostolic authority. Acting in the name of Christ's Church, he invites them to write their names in the Book of the Elect. Consider the seriousness of what is being done here!

Individual believers have discerned, in good conscience, that God is calling them to commit their lives to Christ in his Church. The Church authenticates the validity of their vocation, and in an act of worship celebrates its faith that their names are written in what the Holy Scriptures call 'The Book of Life'. They have been chosen by God. Shall we dismiss this as pious play-acting, or shall we see it as nothing less than an act of divine faith? It is an assertion in concrete visible actions, of something believed by the gift of faith.

Yes, it is true, the Almighty and most Holy God is indeed acting, here and now, in the life of you, whoever you are, whatever your name, and has called and chosen you for a life of communion with him that is his gift to you in Jesus Christ. The Rite of Election expresses a person's commitment to the purification and enlightenment that prepares the heart for the Sacraments of Easter: Baptism, Confirmation and Holy Eucharist.

## RENEWED IN OUR SENSE OF BEING CALLED AND CHOSEN

If you have persevered this far, you are reading this book by choice. For whatever reasons – entirely personal to you, you decided to give it a go and you have continued in your choice. The decision to give consideration to all that is proposed here has taken place within the context of your choice, made over many years, to continue seeking to be loyal to your Christian calling. In other words, one way or another, however recently or however long ago, you have chosen to respond to God's call by living by faith in Jesus Christ. Indeed, as an expression of this repeatedly renewed choice, you have celebrated the renewal of Baptismal Promises each Easter and probably at other times too.

In a sense, therefore, there is nothing 'new' at all in what this book is inviting you to do. There is, on the other hand, something entirely new. That we may be open to this 'new thing,' it was said earlier that we must look for, pray for, hope for and, more importantly than anything else *expect the Lord to give you* a renewed *'sense of the mystery'* in which you have been involved all these years. In the same way that the confirmation candidates were quite aware of their own actions in deciding to ask for confirmation, you will be quite aware of what it has actually meant to you to decide to lead a Christian life. This awareness is not the object of our faith. The object of our faith is what God has been doing in all this.

Turn inside out your own history of Christian discipleship. Look at it not from the point of view of all that you have put into it; look rather at all that God has been putting into it. At the very least, all that God has been doing is as real as all that you have been doing. Ask the Lord, with an expectant faith, to give you a new sense of all that he has been doing to bring about this moment in your life. Ask him for a renewed sense, not an idea in your mind, but a heart-felt touch, a spiritual sense of what is actually going on that you should want to live out all that it means to be a baptised, confirmed, communicating member of the Body of Christ. Ask the Lord to open the ears of our hearts that you may hear those words he speaks to us as he spoke to the disciples on the night before he died.

"It was not you who chose me, but I who chose you and appointed you to go and bear fruit that will remain, so that whatever you ask the Father in my name he may give you."[10]

In a commentary on these words I read: "It was not that by nature they were more inclined than others to seek God, or that they had any native goodness to recommend them to him, but it was because he graciously inclined them by his Holy Spirit to seek him; because, in the language of the Episcopal and Methodist articles of religion, 'The grace of Christ prevented them;' that is, went before them, commenced the work of their personal salvation, and thus God in sovereign mercy chose them as His own."[11] This 'going before us', this coaxing us on is what is asked of the Holy Spirit in the Lenten process of purification and enlightenment.

In the months prior to next Lent and Easter, we celebrate the Advent and Christmas Liturgy. During that time pray that your heart may be open to the wonder of what we said earlier about the meaning of the Sacrament or Mystery of Faith: something hidden from all eternity in the bosom of the Father is now made manifest on earth by the appearance of Jesus Christ. If Christ was ever in the bosom of the Father, so were we. "He chose us in him, before the foundation of the world, to be holy and without blemish before him."[12] Prayerful reflection on this word is bound to bring out in us a deep sense of our having been called and chosen for the grace in which we stand. It is the role of evangelists and catechists to bring people already seeking God in darkness, to this realisation: he is not only calling them to himself. He is calling them to himself by calling them into the visible community of faith which celebrates the sacraments of Christ's redeeming presence in the world. Here is God's eternal truth about who each person is, revealed and brought about in Jesus Christ.

It may be that hitherto we have entertained in our minds the idea of Christian vocation but have feared to think seriously about it. What will it cost? What shall I have to give up? Maybe another kind of fear has ruled us. Perhaps what we have known in our minds we have kept at arm's length as something too great to imagine that it could be true for the likes of us. Now is the time to pray for a new sense, a new awakening of the heart to the truth that we may well have been too afraid to embrace so closely. We must pray for the gift of Wisdom which enables us to know in our hearts something hitherto hidden from them: "We speak God's wisdom, mysterious, hidden, which God predetermined before the ages for our glory."[13] God invites us to live in a truth which will reveal to us who we are to God and how in Christ, crucified and risen, how in the sacraments of Jesus Christ, we are brought very close to the God who has longed from all eternity to hold us in this embrace: "God chose to make known the riches of the glory of this mystery among the Gentiles; it is Christ in you, the hope for glory."[14]

## THE BOOK OF THE ELECT

Those of us baptised in infancy never chose to enter our names in the Book of the Elect. However, I know that before I was ordained deacon and priest, I signed on the dotted line as will all who have been married: people sign the marriage register when they make a life commitment. Catechumens express their commitment in precisely this way when asking for Baptism.

We, who are asking, after many years, perhaps, to be renewed in matters fundamental to our Christian way of life, could do well to remember this: Catechumens are not invited to take the step of entering their names at the beginning of their discipleship. The Rite of Election occurs towards the end of the long preparation. After a period of enquiry and assent to the Gospel of Christ, they are allowed to enrol and enter the Catechumenate. This period of Christian formation will certainly last more than one year and may last several. Eventually, by God's grace, the day will come when they are judged to have so faithfully engaged in the process of Christian formation that they are allowed to apply for the Sacraments of Christian Initiation on Easter Night, by entering their names in the Register of the Elect. Only after a long formation are they called forward on the First Sunday of Lent and chosen for this grace, entering their names as a sign of their commitment to the Lord Jesus Christ and their belief in his first commitment to them.

During the six weeks of Lent they are to pray with the whole community that they may become more and more purified of any obstacles that prevent their being totally open to all that God offers them in their Christian Initiation, to become more enlightened about the depths of the mystery of faith they are to be sharers in. They do not go to Confession but they must confess in their hearts. They have to face up to deep needs which the Lord will enable them to own. God may well expose to their willing hearts some pretty nasty wounds that need healing. They must not hide from what the Lord enables them to see. The grace of their election enables them to repent and accept God's free gift of healing.

In preparing to renew our Baptismal Promises, we too may make a new commitment to the work of opening our hearts to a renewal of the graces once given in our Christian Initiation. We can make a new submission to the Holy Spirit working within us to expose to our minds and hearts those attachments we harbour which obstruct the flow of God's grace within us. We can pray with confidence that the Lord will enlighten us, according to our individual, personal needs, in order that we may yield more totally to his grace. Our Christian formation has been going on for years. By shifting our focus from ourselves and all that we have done to correct our faults, by focusing now on the object of our faith, what God is doing, we can take a life-changing step in the pilgrimage of faith. Christian Initiation offers Catechumens freedom from all sin and the beginning of a new life, life in the Spirit of Christ. Our re-focusing on all that was offered us in our Baptism, Confirmation and Communion in the Sacrifice of Christ, can be as life-changing for us today as Christian Initiation is for Catechumens who have thoroughly embraced the forty days of Purification and Enlightenment. We just have to choose it, with an expectant faith.

Where a group prepares together for Easter, our having been chosen for the grace in which we stand can be celebrated in an act of worship. After offering the Lord our praise and listening to his word, the group can sign their names as an act of faith in all God has already done in our pilgrimage of faith and an act of trust in all he will yet accomplish. The action can be an act of faith and thanksgiving: if we have been seeking the Lord, it is only because he first sought us and actually captured our hearts. It can be an expression of our joy that the Lord has found us. By his grace, we have given our assent to his choosing us and he can produce the abundant fruit he has promised will spring from this mutual commitment. We can sign our names as an expression of our responsibility towards a Lord of such graciousness.

# AN ACT OF WORSHIP

## A Hymn

### Opening Prayer:
Father, you created the human race and are the author of our renewal. Bless all your adopted children and bless this group gathered in the desire to be granted a new and profound sense of the mystery of grace into which you have called us. As true children of the promise, may we rejoice in eternal life won, not by the power of nature but through the mystery of your grace. We ask this through Christ our Lord.

### Liturgy of the Word: First Sunday of Lent. Year 'A'

### Intercessions:
Looking forward with an expectant faith that the Lord will renew us in all the gifts once given in our being chosen for Christian Initiation, we pray:
**Lord, hear the prayers of those you have called and chosen.**

We pray that we may fruitfully employ the months ahead that through self-denial and works of holiness, we may be renewed by God's Gift at the Easter Festival.
**Lord, hear the prayers of those you have called and chosen.**

That we may grow in a profound sense that God has chosen us, before the foundation of the world, for the grace in which we stand through our Christian Initiation.
**Lord, hear the prayers of those you have called and chosen.**

We pray for all who are not yet baptised, that with us they may yield to the purifying action of the Spirit, opening their hearts to the outpouring of his grace.
**Lord, hear the prayers of those you have called and chosen.**

We pray for each and for all members of this group that supporting each other in daily prayer we may rejoice in God's faithfulness at Easter.
**Lord, hear the prayers of those you have called and chosen.**

We ask the intercession of Mary, that we may share the grace of responding to God's election call as she did: Hail, Mary….

In Jesus we see revealed all that God has chosen us to share. Let us confidently pray in the words he gave us:
Our Father…

Father of love and power, it is your will to establish everything in Christ and to draw us into his all-embracing love. Guide all whom you have called and chosen to become members of your Church; strengthen them in their vocation, build them into the kingdom of your Son and renew in them all that was promised in the seal by which they were sealed in the outpouring of the Spirit of your promise. Hear our prayer through Christ our Lord. Amen

## A Blessing and a Hymn

# CHAPTER THREE

# PURIFIED

## WHAT DOES GOD CALL ME FROM? WHAT DOES HE FREE ME FROM?

St. Paul, in the Letter to the Romans describes something going on in the depths of each person's heart which any honest person will recognise. "What I do, I do not understand. For I do not do what I want but I do what I hate…. The willing is ready at hand but doing the good is not. For I do not do the good I want, but I do the evil I do not want. Miserable one that I am! Who will deliver me from this?[1] The Apostle speaks to us of this hopelessness, not as an abstract analysis of the human condition in general, he speaks from personal experience. He describes what he sees in himself as the reality of things even though this same person also said of himself, "in righteousness based on the law, I was blameless."[2]

Desperate though his plight may be if left to his own devices, he is no longer overwhelmed by a sense of helplessness in the face of the mystery of sin. He proclaims his faith in God's answer to his need, "Thanks be to God through Jesus Christ our Lord." If we are able to share Paul's acceptance of his situation without Christ and if we come to share his faith in the deliverance Christ brings, we shall be able to share the thanks he offers God. Thanking God through Jesus Christ our Lord is the act of worship offered by those who have accepted Christian Initiation. Baptism and Confirmation are completed by the Thanksgiving, the *Eucharist* of the Lord Jesus Christ which our Christian Initiation empowers us to offer. Mass is the Church's central act of worship which we take part in weekly, or perhaps, daily. If we are to come to a real sense of thanksgiving, it can only be by coming first to a profound sense of our need. We need to crawl before we can walk. It is this first part of the Paschal Journey to which we now turn.

The Catechumenate prepares people to discover the reality and the power of God's grace at work in them through Baptism, Confirmation and Holy Eucharist. However, our hearts cannot be open to what the Lord wants to bring about in us, if we have no real sense of our need for what He offers. "It is not those who are healthy who need a physician, but those who are sick; I did not come to call the righteous, but sinners."[3]

We cannot easily ignore a broken leg or an abscess behind our teeth. Sicknesses more hidden from our senses are more easily denied. You may have had the experience of seeing someone greatly loved whose life seems to be falling apart. You may have longed to say, "You must see someone about it." All too often the reply is an angry, "There is nothing wrong with me. I am just going through a bad patch." People behave like this when confronted with an emotional or psychological illness. How much more in the dark we can be about our spiritual ailments.

An essential element in the revelation that God has made to mankind in Jesus Christ is the news, shocking to us, that all mankind is sick. It is floundering around in the dark about its real relationship to our Creator. The more we are determined to look after ourselves without *turning* to the only one who can heal his creation, the more blind we become to our predicament. Remember the words of the Lord Jesus to the Pharisee who did not see the power of love in the woman he regarded as outside the law. "I tell you, her many sins have been forgiven; hence, she has shown great love. But the one to whom little is forgiven, loves little."[4] We do not have to have lived a life of vicious hatred, a life of uncaring deceit, or self-centred debauchery, to own up to our real situation. This, after all, was not the history of Saul of Tarsus. We do need to recognise in ourselves the roots of what in other circumstances may have grown out of control, and produced in abundance its destructive flower and fruit. "There," we say very piously, "but for the grace of God go I." Yet, it is something we have to believe – and believe it as the Word of God to us!

The Catechumenate should bring us to realise this is not a pious thought; it is a fundamental *fact of life*. It may well be that God's providence, manifested in a Christian upbringing, which the Lord graciously offered us through the faith of others, has preserved us from the grosser manifestations of human evil. However, we are still living in the dark if we have not yet realised that we are no different from any other human being and that we are capable of anything.

The prayerful reflection on our situation without Christ, which these words are intended to evoke, should bring us to the same point that the Catechumenate is intended to bring the, as yet, un-baptised. It is intended to lead us to make such a renewal of our baptismal commitment to the Lord Jesus Christ as we expect from those making this commitment for the first time. The Lord will certainly bring the Catechumens to a profound experience of his grace in their lives if they will allow him to lead them into a real sense of their need. In the same way he will lead us to a *renewal* of all that was first offered us in our own Christian Initiation, if we allow him to lead us into a renewed sense of our need. I call it, 'square one of the Gospel'.

To have a profound sense of our *need* is not the Gospel which brings us salvation; it is the place we need to come to if we are to be flooded with the grace the Gospel brings. The sense of standing under God's just judgement, the sense of our being outside God's grace without Christ, these are ways of speaking about the hold that sin has on us without all that God has done for us in Christ. Our sense of wonder at the mystery of the grace in which we now stand, will be commensurate with our sense of the mystery of alienation from God from which we have been liberated. As the hymn says,

> "T'was grace that taught my heart to fear
> And grace my fear relieved."[5]

One of the gifts of the Holy Spirit is called 'courage'. The Spirit led Jesus into a forty day confrontation with sin. The same Spirit will lead us to profound purification of heart if we will accept from him the courage to face up to our deepest wounds, our deepest need for healing. Our readiness to make this journey can be a true act of hope, that is to say, the confidence in God which accompanies faith and charity. We may be utterly confident that he who leads us to confront sin, is He who will lead us on to that place where we join the whole Eucharistic community in saying, "We thank you that you have counted us worthy to stand in your presence and serve you."[6]

We speak of our Christian Initiation as a sharing in the Paschal Mystery of Christ: going down in to the tomb with him to be raised to *a new way of living* through the Resurrection. The Paschal Mystery has, therefore, both a bright side and a dark side, and the way to the bright side is by willingly entering the dark side. Does the prospect of coming face to face with all that is not of God within us fill us with fear? If so, remember that the Lord Jesus has come into our lives not as our judge, but as our Redeemer.

If we are still fearful of the grip sin has on us and of looking at it straight in the eye, remember that the Lord Jesus does not require us to go where he himself has not been! He invites us to *follow* and he assures us, "If you remain in my word you will truly be my disciples and you will know the truth and the truth will set you free."[7] The one who invites us to look within ourselves and to accept our need to be freed from sin, asks only that we look at our own sinfulness. He does not ask us to take upon ourselves the sins of the entire world as he did. However, meditating upon the Lord Jesus in the Garden of Gethsemane, there may enter the secret places of our hidden self a heart-breaking truth. Seeing him ready to take upon himself the sins of all the world, we may see him lifting from ourselves and taking upon himself the burden of all that each of us has done to defile God's beloved creation. The Lord Jesus is my Saviour because he has gone, on my behalf, to that place where my sins would have taken me, left to myself. He has risen from it and invites me to let him lift me up.

The prophet said, "Rend your hearts, not your garments, and return to the Lord, your God. For gracious and merciful is he, slow to anger, rich in kindness and relenting in punishment."[8] When we let the power of God's word break our stony hearts, there can be no doubt that the Lord will fulfil the promise made through another of his prophets, "I will give you a new heart and place a new spirit within you; taking from your bodies your stony hearts and giving you natural hearts."[9]

We do not have to undergo the task which was his, of taking away the sin of the world. But we do at least have to embrace the truth of our absolute need that he should do so. In the Letter to the Hebrews, Jesus, crucified and risen, is described as our High Priest who has once and for all entered the Holy of Holies to intercede for us and we are invited to put all our trust in him. Why should we be ready to trust him when perhaps we have been let down by others? Because he does not speak to us from Olympian heights of greatness far removed from our humble existence. We may allow the Spirit of the Lord Jesus to lead us because he knows from experience what it is like for us. "We do not have a high priest who is unable to sympathize with our weaknesses, but one who has similarly been tested in every way, yet without sin."[10]

It is this Jesus, brought low by the weight of sin in the Garden of his agony who said to his disciples, and to us, not in condemnation but in sympathy, "The spirit is willing but the flesh is weak."[11] We must let the grace of Christ enable us to embrace the truth of our weakness, and perhaps the best way of opening our heart to this grace is to focus on him, in the garden, facing mankind's dead-end destiny, sharing all that is ours that we may share all that is his. We can never meditate enough on the readiness of Jesus, sinless though he was, to place himself before the Father bearing all the consequences of sharing in our humanity. When on the cross, he said, "Into your hands, I commend my spirit" he placed himself precisely where you and I are, that is to say, wholly subject to God's justice, relying utterly on God's mercy, the loving kindness in which God has ever held his estranged children.

If we persist in living by the Law, as St. Paul describes it, we shall continue in the illusion that what God looks for in us is good behaviour, which seeing, he will reward. St. Paul came to realise, once he came to know the Lord Jesus Christ, that when God looks upon us, he sees his beloved hopelessly entangled in the mystery of sin, mankind without God, Godlessness. His response, in Jesus, is to enter this mystery and graciously lead us out of it. He looks to us only for that humble and contrite heart which Jesus, on first proclaiming the Gospel of salvation asked, "Repent and believe in the Gospel."[12] – Square one of the Gospel!

To follow the Lord's invitation into this place of repentance, will lead us into the place described in the Book of Genesis. The mythological description of sin's origin describes not a geographical place in the history of mankind but the 'place' deep within ourselves where, if we let the Lord lead us there, will expose us to our nakedness and to God's response, in Christ, to our predicament. The Book of Genesis describes only the *promise* of the one to come. Jesus crucified and risen reveals the fulfilment of that promise. Later on we shall consider the wonder of having 'put on Christ', of having been 'clothed in Christ' in whom mankind is restored to God's image and likeness. For the present, let us remain at the point of promise.

Our divine vocation, God's invitation to us to live by faith, is never an event in the past, over and done with. It is the ever present foundation of our relationship with God in Christ. In the same way, our call to recognise our situation without this grace, is an ever-present defence against any foolish notion that we have some claim on God's justice because of good works. The Genesis story, if we are able to recognise it as our own, will enable us to realise that so dreadful is our entanglement in sin, that on hearing God's call our immediate reaction is to *hide*. The perniciousness of sin, in its deepest roots, causes us to *pass a judgement on God*. Our sinful instinct is a fear that springs from a lie.

In the story, mankind, hitherto, has known nothing but blessings from God, but having got himself into a situation not of God, he is terrified of standing before Him, because *he has nothing of his own making*; he fears being totally exposed. He has to hear God who created him naked and, hitherto, has given all that he needed for his well-being, asking him, "Who told you you were naked?" What did God ever expect of mankind? What did he demand? What did mankind have to bring that was not God's gift? The undoing of this lie about God's attitude to us has to be undone by faith in who *God* says he is and who we are to him. We have to be freed from the imprisonment of the lies we have believed about God and ourselves. For us, entangled in the mystery of sin in our origins, this faith must be the expression of a humble, contrite heart. It must be a faith in the freedom that God, in his loving kindness, offers his estranged children, a faith that God has never wanted anything else.

Catholic Tradition understands the liberation from sin and the new birth brought about by Baptism rather differently from some Protestant traditions. Some, perhaps describing themselves as 'evangelical,' see human nature as totally corrupted by sin and faith as the 'covering' that clothes our nakedness. God attributes to us a justification that is not ours but Christ's. The impression can be given that with the decision to accept faith in Christ, to accept one's hopelessness without him and to admit Jesus into one's life as Lord and Saviour, salvation is accomplished and assured. Our justification before God is accomplished by that decision in faith.

Our Catholic faith teaches otherwise. There has to be a radical turning away from sin and a radical embrace of God's enabling grace. Our full conversion to this truth and grace takes a lifetime. This is because we do not see God's beloved creation as totally corrupted and 'clothed over'. On the contrary we regard the mystery of grace as actually *undoing sin's effects and restoring from within our human nature the image and likeness once lost*. We may well have been delivered from the power of sin, but we have also been radically restored to a living relationship with God. A new beginning has been brought about in us and now, in the power of God's grace, we are enabled to carry out good works. These are not something we do in our own power. They are the authentic fruits of that fount of grace into which we have been drawn: the Christ in whom we now live, by the power of the Spirit. By the power of this re-creating grace we become co-authors with our creator-redeemer in the growth of the Reign of God.

There is an ancient catechetical tradition which sees *human pride* as sin's root in us. However, there is more than one way of thinking about this pride, something deeper than human understanding. For St. Augustine, preaching at the end of the 4th century, the origin of sin was the deliberate, free action of a mature human being – an imitation of the angelic "I will not serve." St. Augustine thought of Adam as being created a mature man who by a deliberate choice ruined his posterity.

St. Irenaeus, preaching in the second century, saw this proud action in a different way. What is described in the mythological language of the Book of Genesis, he saw more as the act of an immature human being. He saw the flaw in us as the kind of thing you see in what we would call a 'wilful child', demanding to be let do on his own what he cannot. Grabbing what he wants before he can appreciate what it really is, he has to suffer the self-inflicted wound of trying to walk before he can crawl; to run before he can walk. In the story of Adam reaching out to the forbidden fruit, I see someone trying to grab for himself what he is too immature to realise will be his as gift, but only when he is mature enough to receive it.

This is not at all the same thing as refusing to accept responsibility for one's actions. We all know what it means, whether as infants, children, adolescents, young men or women, middle-aged and, God help us, even old people, to act on the blinding impulse, *"I want it and I want it now!"* Our frustrated tantrums did not come to an end in the nursery. I do not see our human pride as imitating Milton's Lucifer. I see it more as an embarrassing, humiliating matter – but with no less dreadful consequences. I think this foolish pride which prevents us seeing just how little we are, also prevents us from believing in the infinite power of God's mercy in the face of the most dreadful human evils. Sin so deludes us about our greatness that we actually believe that our capacity for wrong-doing is greater than God's capacity or readiness to forgive. That is the real blindness of stupid, infantile human pride. If we persist in living 'on our own' in this way, not needing God's enabling help, we are on a hiding to nowhere, wilful children, stubbornly refusing to be cuddled. We shall most certainly end up on our own unrelated to 'the Lord, the giver of life': dead.

God in Christ offers us freedom from this dead end. We enter this freedom by opening our hearts to his free gift. He has to bring us to the point where we realise that we can bring nothing but our contrite hearts and that God has never wanted anything else from his estranged children. We have to give up wanting to save ourselves. We have to give up insulting the one who keeps offering us all that is needed, in the illusion that we don't need it; we can do it on our own.

Because our liberation from sin is a new creation, we can always be renewed in its power by coming to its source. This we do in a special way each year when the worship of the whole Church celebrates those "events that gave us new life in Christ" – the Paschal Mystery of Christ's death and resurrection and the sacraments of faith by which we were incorporated into it.

## POINTS FOR FAITH SHARING

Paul lived a very dutiful Jewish life.
The mistake he made was to imagine this
put him 'in God's good books'. Meeting
the Lord Jesus Christ destroyed this illusion.
It may be that we have lived a dutiful 'Catholic' life.
Where do I stand in the matter?


St. John says, "The Law was given through Moses
but grace has come through our Lord Jesus Christ."
What did he mean?


Am I afraid of admitting, to myself and before God:
"I am not a sinner because I commit sins.
I commit sins because I am sinful."
i.e. I am prone to sin.

# AN ACT OF WORSHIP

## A Hymn

### Opening Prayer:
Father, we rejoice that your all-powerful Word has broken through the crust of our sins and awakened in our hearts the desire to respond wholly to your grace. Grant us the wisdom to accept your truth about our need for your mercy and truth about the freedom of the forgiveness you offer. We make our prayer etc.

### Old Testament Reading: Hosea, 11.
(The Lord's abiding love in the face of infidelity)

### New Testament Reading: Rom. 3, 21-20
(Justification through faith in Christ)

### Gospel: Matt. 11. 25-30

### Intercessions:
We believe that God who has created us has done so for no other reason than that we should share his life. As the gateway to this destiny restored to us in Jesus, crucified and risen, he invites us to open our hearts to his gift of forgiveness. We pray:
**Lord grant us a humble and contrite heart.**

We come before Him who created us in his own image and

likeness and gladly confess we have lived in what St. Augustine called, "the land of unlikeness". That the way home may be open to us, we pray:
**Lord grant us a humble and contrite heart.**

St. John says, "If we say 'We are without sin,' we deceive ourselves, and the truth is not in us."[13] That we may be freed from sin's blindness we pray:
**Lord grant us a humble and contrite heart.**

The Pharisee praised God that he was not like the rest of men. So that with the publican we may gladly confess that we are, we pray:
**Lord grant us a humble and contrite heart.**

When Zachaeus realised Jesus wished to come into his home, he was able to turn away from sin; that we too may renounce sin and welcome Jesus into every area of our lives, let us pray:
**Lord grant us a humble and contrite heart.**

We honour the power of God's grace in Mary, preserving her from all sin and ask her motherly prayer: Hail Mary…

Since we have in Jesus a high priest who intercedes for us and is able to sympathise with us in weakness, being like us in all things but sin, we pray confidently in the words he gave us: Our Father…

Father, we believe that you have never ceased to call all mankind to yourself and now, in Jesus crucified and risen, you have opened for us the way for our return. Take away our hearts of stone and, according to your promise, made though the prophet Ezekiel, give us a heart of flesh; touch us there with the two-edged sword of your word that will set us free to live with you. We make our prayer etc.

## A Blessing and a Hymn

## THE FIRST AND SECOND SCRUTINIES

The Rite of Election having taken place on the First Sunday of Lent, there takes place on the Third, Fourth and Fifth Sundays of Lent acts of worship called 'The Scrutinies'. The English word suggests that those preparing for baptism are being publicly scrutinised by the community. Are they ready 'to become one of us'? This, however, is not so.

If the Elect have been the subject of external scrutiny, that is to say, if they have been subjected to an assessment made by church leaders that they are ready to go forward to baptism, such a scrutiny has already happened. Church leaders, seeking the guidance of the Spirit, made a scrutiny of those applying for baptism, as a result of which they were permitted to write their names in the Book of the Elect. The scrutiny which the whole community prays for on behalf of the Elect, these Sundays of Lent, is altogether different.

The Church prays that the Elect will recognise and embrace the infinitely delicate but all-powerful heart searching in which the Holy Spirit must guide them in the secrecy of their individual hearts. This must happen so that all obstacles, particular to each human heart, will be acknowledged and submitted to the redeeming power of the Saviour in the sacraments of Christian Initiation. The spiritual nature of the scrutinies, the spiritual author of the scrutinies and the spiritual outcome of the scrutinies cannot be over-emphasised.

The meaning of the Scrutinies is described in R.C.I.A. *"The Scrutinies are rites for self-searching and repentance and have above all a spiritual purpose. They are meant to uncover then heal all that is weak, defective or sinful in the hearts of the elect; to bring out, then strengthen all that is upright, strong and good. The scrutinies are celebrated in order to deliver the elect from the power of sin and Satan, to protect them against temptation, and to give them strength in Christ who is the way, the truth and the life.*

*"The elect must have the intention of achieving an intimate knowledge of Christ and his Church and they are expected to progress in genuine self-knowledge through serious examination of their life and true repentance.*

*"First of all the elect are instructed gradually about the mystery of sin, from which the whole world and every person longs to be delivered and thus saved from its present and future consequences. Second, their spirit is filled with Christ the Redeemer who is the living water, the light of the world, and the resurrection and the life.*

*"In the rite of exorcism the elect are freed from the effects of sin and from the influence of the devil. They receive new strength in the midst of their spiritual journey and they open their hearts to receive the gifts of the Saviour."*[14]

These acts of worship, prayers and blessings for deliverance from the power of sin take place after the proclamation of three Gospel stories. The Elect are invited to take to heart the stories of Jesus and the woman at the well, Jesus and the man born blind and Jesus rescuing Lazarus from the power of death. These are three of the signs which the Gospel according to John gives us, "that you may believe that Jesus is the Christ, the Son of God, and that by believing you may have life in his name."[15] They should be the focus of our reflection and prayer as we seek to discover what the Scrutinies might mean for our own lives and how we may enjoy the blessings they offer in preparing to renew our baptismal promises.

These signs offer abundant insights for our meditation. The first is that the choice of these three stories for the liturgy of the Scrutinies seems to suggest progress, movement from one level of perception to another. The stories start from the need to confront the consequences of personal choice. This is absolutely necessary in any process of conversion. The second story leads us to recognise we are in a situation into which we were born, a pre-volitional situation; we are involved in something deeper than personal choice. The third story invites us to accept the fact that only through a personal relationship with Jesus Christ can we be liberated, lifted out of the enduring consequences of this pre-volitional predicament.

## THE MYSTERY OF SIN – APPROACHING THE REALITY FROM WHERE WE ACTUALLY ARE

R.C.I.A. says that if we are going to let the Spirit guide us in a spiritual self-searching that leads to repentance and a healing of what is weak and defective in our sinful hearts, we had better start off from the right place: instruction about the mystery of sin. In a sense R.C.I.A. recognises that we need no introduction for, as it says, we are dealing with something within us which all the world knows we would be better off without. Just what is it? We can begin by looking at the difference between *feeling uneasy about being in the wrong* and courageously standing before God, accepting **his word** that there is something about us which is not of Him. We can *feel* guilty, remorseful, a failure, unworthy. We can also recognise that we are morally responsible for something without feeling anything of the kind. A sense of moral responsibility is the fruit of conscience; self-accusatory feelings are a psychological response to feeling unsure of ourselves.

Just what is this something about us which, whatever we feel, we can honestly say is unlike God? It wouldn't take much soul-searching to admit, "It always involves putting ourselves first doesn't it?" When we put ourselves first whether it is in place of something or someone we know has a prior claim on our attention, something tells us, if we are trying live in the truth, we are in the wrong. We can put ourselves first for many reasons or, more usually, because of feelings we have towards others. Sometimes we deliberately choose to turn away from somebody's right or their need for our attention. Sometimes our self-centred act occurs less by deliberate choice than a habit of putting our own comfort first – an indifference, a lack of interest, maybe an unawareness of the needs or even the rights of others.

In learning to recognise the mystery of sin at work in us, we must learn to acknowledge the humiliating truth of just how un-free we can be. In my childhood, I gained the impression that to commit a mortal sin was as easy as falling off a log. However, even as I picked up that impression, the very theological language which defined it said that to 'fall' into mortal sin is precisely what we cannot do. To fall, whether that means tripping over the kerb, or plunging headlong down a cliff, means we are not in control. However, mortal sin meant an action (or an omission!) strictly defined as *deliberate*. The word means something well-considered and freely chosen something the courts would describe as a 'pre-meditated crime.' By definition, therefore, it excluded all human activities – however damaging their consequences, that are undertaken when a person is 'swept away', as we would say, by intense emotion or passion. To use the language of modern psychology, when a person can be in the grip of a complex which renders them un-free in a particular area of human conduct.

All these things, and much more besides, have to be taken into account when it comes to assessing our *moral responsibility* for our behaviour. Even when we are making *choices,* for which we know we are responsible, we can be swayed by a multitude of reasons or *feelings* in regard to others. If we are indeed, rational animals, (another definition in the theological language of our upbringing) it does not mean that our reasoning process is always, or for that matter, usually unaffected by emotions. The very opposite is true. We are never going to be able to come face to face with the mystery of sin if we have too high an estimate of our human capacity for free choice in all that we do. To claim that humans have free will does not mean that they exercise it all the time or, indeed, that many people exercise it a lot of the time.

If we are honest, it is probably true to say that if we were brought up in a very Christian environment, we grew up with a pretty high demand on our developing moral sense. However, there was not a corresponding acceptance of just how weak and fragile human beings can actually be. As a consequence, what we would call our 'moral outlook' may have made us harsh judges of ourselves and, because of this, others, including God. Pursuing the high moral goals the Law pointed to may have led us to a deep disappointment with ourselves for our failures. This may have led us to believe that our *self*-condemnation in falling short of our aims was conscience – God's response to our sinfulness. This is a defence mechanism called *projection*. If we imagine God judges us in the way we judge ourselves, we imagine we can placate him by *feeling guilty* – crying, like a child, over spilt milk.

God, in his wisdom, may well have preferred us to be more like him and less selfish. However, being wise, He has an understanding of the mystery of sin which we lack. Perhaps, realistically, He *expected less* of our human weakness than we, in our pride, assumed ourselves capable of. Without knowing it, we may be less rational than we thought ourselves to be in assessing our moral responsibility. Our judgements about ourselves and the seriousness of our sins, can be clouded by *feelings* of guilt. *Feelings* of failure, *feelings* of unworthiness can be mistaken for our conscience. It has been said that we are so devious that we are perfectly capable of *feeling* guilty about matters in which our moral responsibility is a lot slighter than we imagine, and have no sense of guilt in matters for which we are seriously responsible. One of the greatest insights into the mystery of sin is that it causes, 'weakness of the will and darkness of the mind'. The human pride from which sin springs blinds us to how little and weak we really are. We are not the masters of the universe we can imagine ourselves to be – however grave the damage we are capable of wreaking on ourselves, on others and the world around us through our immature behaviour.

## SELF-DISCIPLINE – ITS GOOD AND BAD EFFECTS

Before proceeding, remember St. Paul's explanation of the role of the Law in our formation. He compared it to the authority of a tutor over someone too immature for personal responsibility. In our moral formation we need the discipline of submitting to parental or tutorial authority. Lacking this in their formative years, people 'fall' into the grip of their emotions and passions. They become victims of deep feelings they have never been asked to learn how to control or *integrate into their personality.* Indeed, for many reasons we cannot go into here, they may become psychologically in the grip of complexes sometimes as strong as their own sense of self: morally un-free in some aspect of human living.

Time was when the life-style of the rich and powerful was hidden from the general population. However, over the last hundred years, literacy, the mass media (which in the first part of the twentieth century meant the gossip columns), the internet, social networks, and the ever expanding world of electronic communication means that the peccadilloes and sometimes the severely harmful lifestyles of the rich and powerful are instantly accessible to the general public. While the mass media exposes something of the glamour of 'celebrity' it also reports its damaging effects. Information about the life-style beyond the means of the vast majority of people sometimes reveals that heirs to a great inheritance, whether this be of super-stars, entrepreneurs, or royalty, simply cannot cope with what is available to them. Access to opportunities becomes access to excess. Freedom without responsibility has actually proved to be the occasion of self- harm or even self-destruction, because they have not found it in themselves to be discreet, balanced, and prudent in their use of what is within their reach.

St. Paul seeing that we have been destined since the foundation of the world to be coheirs with Christ, saw that the purpose of the Law was to discipline people too immature to appreciate who they were, by God's grace, and that all that they had at their disposal was gift. It is the same insight that gives meaning to the Catechumenate. This period in Christian Formation is necessary before we are baptised as adults and if we were baptised in infancy it still has to take place. It is an apprenticeship in the freedom of the children of God given us in Christian Initiation and something that cannot be side-stepped.

## GRADUAL LEARNING – GOD'S RESPECT FOR OUR LITTLENESS

R.C.I.A., in addition to its emphasis on learning to confront the mystery of sin by starting off from the right place, also shows a deep respect for the kind of people we are by stressing that our introduction must be gradual. While this introduction must include information, something that enlightens our minds, it must, more importantly, lead us to realise that something is *infecting* us spiritually, and for this a gentle hand and voice is needed. Our introduction to the mystery of sin should be less a lecture on ethics than a consultation about our personal state of health.

In the same way that having detected signs of ill-health in ourselves we consult a specialist to find out what is going on, R.C.I.A. must help us to recognise the reality of our condition and introduce us to the Healer who can and will sort it out. For immature people, sin can only be perceived as breaking rules imposed upon us by a stronger will. Conversion, in this case, is little more than submission – even when this submission recognises the validity of the Law's claim. It requires a certain amount of maturity and humbleness of heart to hear, not a policeman or a head teacher upbraiding us for being in the wrong, but a doctor who has to break the news to us that we are terminally sick – something we did not personally choose – like the man born blind.

'In the fullness of time' when God, in Jesus Christ, revealed the plan entertained in his heart 'before the foundation of the world' his first task was to enlighten our minds that without Him, we are on a hiding to nowhere. We are alienated from the goal, the purpose, for which God created us. If we do things that something within us tells us is not of God, the first thing this should teach us is that we are not totally outside the power of God's Word to touch us. If we attend to this word, we are already responding to Truth and responding to God's grace. This is so, even if we do not know the origin of this word in the One God, Living and True who has a purpose for all mankind as yet historically undisclosed to us. When we do come to some knowledge of God's eternal plan, we must as a first step, "Turn aside from the way we see things (repent) and *believe the good news*" This good news says that Christ has come among us as our physician, the healer of the human predicament.

Sin is not something that begins with our choices. Our choices for wrongdoing - however mixed up they may be with feelings, emotions and passions – spring from our involvement in something we did *not cause* in ourselves, although the more readily we yield to its drawing power, the more we become un-free to make good choices. It is certainly the case that *in dealing* with the mystery of sin, we must *begin* at the level of personal, conscious, deliberate choices. However, if we allow the Spirit to guide us, as the Scrutinies pray, we shall be led to the less conscious manifestations of sin and ultimately to its pre-volitional origin in us.

It requires some humility of heart to stand before God in a deep acceptance of this word. God has to lead us to this point gradually. Because we are so insecure, we need the gift of faith to be comfortable with the truth that God simply wants us to come to him as we really are. Where we come from is not the primary issue. The Lord may have called us from the slavery to his own self-indulgence of the prodigal son, who abandoned his father. Equally, it may have been the rule-keeping, wage-earning servitude of the elder one who seems never to have realised he was a beloved son. We all need to be coaxed into living in the defenceless, naked truth. Why do we need this gentle hand? Because even when we imagine ourselves to be the world's biggest sinner, it gives us in our pride, some special claim of our own to hang on to!

## WAS JESUS SPEAKING THE TRUTH ON THE CROSS?

There is a word in Holy Scripture which always catches me in the throat. It gently upbraids us for our incredulity when confronted by the power of God's love in our regard. It is the word spoken to Sarah by the three visitors to Abraham's tent. They come to assure the Patriarch that his faith in God has not been misplaced and that he will indeed receive the child of promise. This is a very great and holy word about God's faithfulness. The promises he made to human beings are the bearers of God's eternal purpose that reaches beyond all that the human heart can imagine is possible. Sarah, hiding behind the tent flap, giggles at the thought that she is to be a mother so late in life. When she realises that the visitors have heard her, she is overcome by embarrassment. "Why did Sarah laugh? Is anything too marvellous for the Lord to do? At the appointed time I will return to you, and Sarah will have a son." Because she was afraid, Sarah dissembled, saying, "I didn't laugh," To this, these emissaries of God's most gracious promise said in gentle but unmistakable reproach, "Yes you did."[16]

In the face of God's promise to a humble and contrite heart, we may not laugh at what may seem absurdly impossible, but we have to ask ourselves just how blindly steeped we are in unbelief. There is a question we may put to ourselves to discover just how deeply we have been moved to believe by the two-edged sword that is the word of God.

Was Jesus speaking about me and my ignorance of what sin has brought about in my life when, on the cross he cried out, "Father, forgive them, they know not what they do."?[17] Is it possible that the boldness of Jesus' words is so great that we think piously, "What a lovely thing to say, Lord," but deep down thinking, "Of course they knew – and so do I"?

In the words of the dying Jesus, we have to hear the Lord saying to each of us that, whatever we may think we know, we have no idea what sin is doing to God's beloved creation. It is only by *believing him* when he says this to us that we can *begin* to open our hearts to the indescribable graciousness of his response to the mystery of sin, and be healed of what we have no power to deal with in its roots. He promises us that he has the power and the will to heal us. He can and will restore us fully to his grace, and having done this, enable us to become truly capable of good works, the fruit of his miracle of grace at work in us.

The Scrutinies are intended to lead the Catechumens to what I have called 'square one of the Gospel', that place where boasting of nothing and afraid of nothing, we stand before the Lord in that nakedness which Adam and Eve in their sin found they could not do. It is from this radical point that our healing begins.

## AN ACT OF WORSHIP

## A Hymn

### Opening Prayer:
Father, we rejoice that you never cease to recall us to yourself, creating in us, by your most tender touch, a contrite and humble heart. Grant that we may never cease to yield to the Spirit's guidance, exposing our hearts to the healing you offer. Hear our prayer through Christ our Lord

## Liturgy of the Word:
Gospels of the Third and Fourth Sundays of Lent Year 'A'

### Intercessions:
Like the woman of Samaria may we review our lives before Christ, acknowledge our sins and, like the man born blind be enlightened by Him.
**Lord, in your mercy, hear our prayer.**

Pondering God's holy Word, day by day, may we be enabled to confess ourselves as sinners and reject all that is displeasing and contrary to Christ.
**Lord, in your mercy, hear our prayer.**

May the Holy Spirit who searches every heart, help us to overcome our weakness through his power, to know the things of God and lead lives that please Him.
**Lord, in your mercy, hear our prayer.**

May the Lord stir up in us a longing for the living water that brings eternal life making us true worshippers of the Father in spirit and truth.
**Lord, in your mercy, hear our prayer.**

Like the man born blind may we discover the unknown presence of our Healer in our lives and open our hearts to his freely offered gift.
**Lord, in your mercy, hear our prayer.**

May we seek to know our Saviour more and more and become faithful witnesses of his redeeming presence in the world.
**Lord, in your mercy, hear our prayer.**

We pray for all who seek some kind of healing in their lives that they find their deliverance in the name of Jesus borne witness to by all who have experienced his grace.
**Lord, in your mercy, hear our prayer.**

We also pray for all whose hearts are hardened against Christ's merciful touch and may the Lord deliver each of us from any resistance to his intimate presence in our lives.
**Lord, in your mercy, hear our prayer.**

We honour the Blessed Virgin Mary who embraced every sign of God's favour praying that we may imitate her open-heartedness that with her we may magnify his name: Hail, Mary....
In silence we ask the Spirit to be our guide on our journey to true repentance.

Jesus has taught us to believe that from however far away his sons and daughters have returned, the Father has only a welcome in his heart. With the confidence this word brings we pray:
Our Father…

God of power, you sent your Son to be our Saviour. Grant that your people seeking to be renewed in all your gifts, who like the woman of Samaria, thirst for living water, may turn to the Lord as they hear his word and acknowledge the sins and weaknesses that weigh them down.

Protect them from vain reliance on self and defend them from the power of Satan.

Free them from the spirit of deceit, so that, admitting the wrong they have done, they may attain purity of heart and advance in the way of salvation. Hear our prayer through Christ our Lord. Amen

*(praying with hand outstretched over the assembly)*

Lord Jesus, you are the fountain for which your people thirst, you are the Master whom they seek. In your presence they dare not claim to be without sin, for you alone are the Holy One of God.

They open their hearts to you in faith, they confess their faults and lay bare their hidden wounds. In your love free them from their infirmities, heal their sickness, quench their thirst and give them peace.

In the power of your name, which we call upon in faith; stand by them now and heal them. Rule over the spirit of evil, conquered by your rising from the dead.

Show those you have chosen the way of salvation that in the Holy Spirit they may be renewed in the gift of worshipping the Father in spirit and in truth, for you live and reign for ever and ever. Amen

Father of mercy, you led the man born blind to the kingdom of light through the gift of faith in your Son. Renew in your people this same gift of faith, free them from the false values that surround and blind them. Set them firmly in your truth, children of the light, staunch and fearless witnesses to the faith. We ask this through Christ our Lord.

## A Blessing and a Hymn

# THE THIRD SCRUTINY

## THE MYSTERY OF GOD'S REPONSE TO THE MYSTERY OF SIN

Having described something of the infinite delicacy by which the Spirit of Truth leads those ready to enter the dark side of the Paschal Mystery, the moment has come to try and indicate something of the infinite delicacy of God's response to sin. The Scrutinies pray that the Spirit will lead the Elect to purification and enlightenment. The mystery of God's grace is infinitely greater than the mystery of sin, however terrible is man's inhumanity to man. In the words of St. Paul, "where sin increased, grace overflowed all the more."[18] In a perfectly ordinary, everyday experience, I was given a new insight into what I thought I already believed.

## IN JESUS, GOD RAISES OUR SIGHTS

This book is based on a catechetical course given in 2011-2012, lasting from late autumn to Lent with a mid winter break from the middle of November till the end of December. During the break I went on holiday to South Africa. During the course of my visit, I contracted an infection which led to septic arthritis. After surgery on my ankle, I lay on my back, in hospital, plugged into a continuous drip of antibiotics and pain-killers. After little more than a week, I had to leave the ward where I had been confined since my admission in order to go to the hospital pharmacy. It was in the hospital's central concourse, and as I was wheeled there, I was struck by the fact that a great wide world existed beyond the place and situation in which I had been living in some kind of suspended animation. There were ordinary, real people all going about their ordinary lives; a great throng entering and leaving the hospital. The reality of a great big world beyond the limited world I had been living in and the only one I had been conscious of for some days, struck me very forcefully.

Advent had already begun when I was taken ill. Each day the Church's Daily Prayer put before me readings from Sacred Scripture and the writings of the Fathers of the Church. As I took them to heart, my focus was being drawn to something already admitted in my mind but as yet not the object of my heart's worship. I already believed that what happened in human history in the life, death and resurrection of Jesus of Nazareth fulfilled God's unique plan for all mankind. This Advent, there began to dawn on me in a new way the truth of our Christian Faith that what was now revealed in human history had an everlasting existence in the heart of God, before the foundation of the world. The revelation was new; the purpose was older than creation. Indeed, there had never been any other plan.

I was particularly drawn to the mysterious reality spoken about in the Advent Liturgy which described Jesus Christ as the 'Desired of the Nations', the object of a desire in people who had never even heard of the promises made by the Lord God of

Israel. The Fourth Gospel and the Letters of John spoke of Jesus as the Word of God already in the world but unrecognised. St Paul wrote of him as embodying all fullness. This year's Advent worship invited me to recognise that the desire in me to live free from the power of sin, was a longing God had implanted in human hearts, deeper than the mystery of sin itself. In Jesus Christ, crucified and risen, God was offering me fulfilment of a gratuitous promise which this longing sought.

As I reflected on this, lying on my hospital bed, I saw mankind from the time of his first creation until the appearing among us of Him of whom God said, "This is my Son, the Beloved. Listen to him." I saw mankind living in some kind of inescapable prison. I thought of the old English Christmas carol, "Adam lay abounden, four thousand years." Knowing of no other kind of existence, we have no real appreciation of our limitations. In my hospital bed, aware only of my need to lie there, I had lost consciousness to a very large extent that the little island of my awareness existed in a great world beyond. It was possible for me to live in my little sin-bound world oblivious of the world of super-abundant grace.

## IN JESUS, GOD REVEALS HIS ENFOLDING LOVE

Outside the pharmacy, I sat in my wheelchair, parked against the wall, waiting for my prescription to be prepared. I watched a great crowd of people passing to and fro, entering and leaving the hospital. Then, someone in the crowd caught my eye. He was an infant, eighteen months to two years old. What struck me first was that I could see his face at the same level as that of the adults passing by. He was sitting in his father's arms rather like one sees in statues where Jesus sits looking out on the world from the lap of the Blessed Virgin. In the case of this child, his father was walking out of the hospital, just one person in a crowd, but with his little boy perched on his left arm and holding him around the tummy with his right arm. The little boy was looking out on the world at the same level as his father's vision.

As he sat there, his father whose head was already quite close to his son's, would lean forward a few inches kissing him repeatedly on the side of his head. How long does it take for a person walking in a crowd of passers-by to come into your sight and pass beyond? However brief a time this was, the father kissed his son several times. I thought that I had never in my life seen such tenderness in one person for another. What a wonderful blessing, I thought, to grow up knowing and responding to such a loving embrace. Then, as they drew nearer, I saw the face of the child more clearly. Was it a little droop on one side of the face? I cannot say, but something about his appearance made me realise with a shock that he was in some way brain damaged.

Then there took place something utterly charming. As they passed me the father noticed a Christmas tree near the wall opposite where I sat. He approached it and let the infant play with the brightly coloured baubles. If this was not enough, he seemed to realise that the wall behind the tree was not smooth and taking his son's little foot drew it across the unevenness of the surface. This caused the child such delight that the father turned, in my direction, towards his wife and smiled at her with the same kind of delight we could all see and hear in his infant son. In some way he had reached the boy who responded to his stimulus. The connection brought joy to both and not only to them but to a total stranger parked in his wheel-chair against the wall.

Back on my bed, reflecting on the beauty of what I had witnessed, I saw mankind, without Christ, one in whom the image or likeness of God had been damaged by the wound of sin. I saw a damaged son, rendered incapable of returning in kind, the tender love the Father never ceased to lavish upon him. Yes, in a certain darkness into which he had been born, mankind could make some response to the God he did not know personally, but this was not the relationship for which God had created us. Just as the infant's father, before the birth of his child, looked forward to a mature, adult, fully developed relationship of father and son, so God had created us. Just like the infant I had seen, mankind is now born into a situation which renders that eventuality impossible. Through what we call the mystery of sin, mankind is born into a situation, not chosen by the individuals now affected by it, in which they can never achieve by their own efforts a healing of their predicament.

As I reflected on the human love, the tenderness, I had seen in the father of the infant, it dawned on me with a clarity never before perceived that the greater the incapacity of his son to respond to his love, the greater was the father's tenderness towards him. As he realised that his son's affliction meant he would never be able to grow into that mature love that can exist between parent and adult offspring, this fact only deepened his tenderness towards his child. In the fatherly love in which he had owned his new-born son, I saw something of the eternal love in which God has ever held me and all mankind. 'Darkness of the mind' is said to be one of sin's primary effects, and in that darkness, to the extent that he entertains any notion of the Divine, mankind makes a terrible, fatal judgement about God.

Our experience of sinfulness makes us feel alien to what we think of as good – sin alienates mankind from God. The insecurity this brings triggers the psychological phenomenon we call *projection* and causes mankind to make the mistake of assuming sin *alienates God from mankind*. In fact, as I had seen in the human love of a father towards his disabled son, the greater our unlikeness to Him who wishes us to be his children, the greater the compassionate tenderness our situation evokes. The greater the sinner I am, the deeper is God's compassionate pity in my regard. Jesus, true image of the Father is, in his life and death, the embodiment of this truth. When the leper said to Jesus of Nazareth, "If you want to, you can cure me," what response did he hope to elicit? I feel sure that he would have been more than happy if Jesus, keeping his distance from one rendered so untouchably unclean by his condition, had, from afar, pronounced him cured. In fact, Mark relates how Jesus did something which must have astonished the recipient of his kindness and horrified those who believed they already knew the mind of God in such matters, "Jesus stretched out his hand and *touched* him, "Of course I want to!" he said, "Be cured"[19]

Once we are aware of this truth revealed in Jesus, how can we possibly fear coming before the Father in all that constitutes our unlikeness to him. Repentance springs from belief in God's true attitude towards our woundedness. In the words of St. Luke, put on the lips of Zachary, father of John the Baptist, "The loving kindness of the heart of our God has dawned upon us bringing light to those who sit in darkness and in the shadow of death, and guiding our feet in the way of peace."[20]

## IN JESUS, GOD REVEALS HIS POWER TO HEAL

While I was overcome by the beauty of the human love I had witnessed and awestruck by what it was saying to me of God's love for us, there dawned on me the difference between the most tender human love and God's love. However much the father I had seen cradling his dear child, wanting him to be aware of his love by his repeated kisses, seeking to stimulate his responses in the delightful things I had witnessed, the father could never hope to do more than to surround his damaged son with his love. He could show his love by protecting him from harm; he could try to reach him in many different ways. The tragic truth is that however great the love, it had no power to heal the brain damage. In this respect the human image falls short of the Divine reality. God's love, unlike human love, has the power and the will to re-create us. As the messengers said in rebuke of Sarah's incredulity, "Is anything too marvellous for the Lord to do?"[21] Sending his son into this world, to share all that is ours that we may share all that is his, God invites us to believe that the power of his creating and redeeming love is infinite. His love for us does have the power to heal us radically. This is the very mystery of grace revealed in Jesus Christ.

## OH, HAPPY FAULT!

The Scrutinies, the whole experience of Lent, leads the Elect to both purification and enlightenment. It is wonderful to believe that however deep our involvement in the mystery of sin, God's only response to our situation is compassion and the deeper our involvement the deeper his compassion. This I saw imaged in the father holding his infant son. It is even more wonderful to believe in the power of God's love revealed in Jesus Christ and now poured out in our hearts by the Gift of the Spirit. In a word, the father I had seen in hospital had no power to deliver his beloved from the predicament into which he was born. God, the Father of our Lord Jesus Christ has done precisely this.

The Easter Faith, celebrated in the Sacraments of Christian Initiation, invites us to believe that sin has been overcome, we have been delivered from all its consequences, we are restored in Christ and in the outpouring of his Holy Spirit, we are now in a living union with the Father. Perhaps these thoughts enable us to realise something of those bold, awesome words the Church sings in the Easter Proclamation:

"Oh happy fault! Oh necessary sin of Adam that gained for us so great a Redeemer."[22]

It is with such an understanding of God's attitude towards all that disfigures us that we should approach the grace for which the scrutinies pray.

## AN ACT OF WORSHIP

## A Hymn

### Opening Prayer:
Father, we come before you that we may be renewed in all that you have done for us in the death and resurrection of your beloved Son. Grant us a new outpouring of your Holy Spirit, that we may be ever more dedicated to the following of Jesus and to proclaiming his holy name. We ask this through Christ our Lord.

### Liturgy of the Word:
Gospel of the Fifth Sunday of Lent. Year 'A'

### Intercessions:
May the Lord awaken in us a new sense of his gifts once given us in the Sacraments of our Christian Initiation when we who were born in sin and destined for death were conformed to Christ in his passion and resurrection.
**Lord, in your mercy, hear our prayer.**

We pray that we may ever live lives of thanksgiving to God who has chosen to rescue us from ignorance of eternal life and set us on the way of salvation.
**Lord, in your mercy, hear our prayer.**

We pray that liberated by repentance from the shackles of sin, we may be renewed in the likeness of Christ, granted us in

Baptism, so that dead to sin we may live for ever in God's sight.
**Lord, in your mercy, hear our prayer.**

Nourished by the Risen Christ in the sacrament of his body and blood may we grow ever closer to the source of life and resurrection.
**Lord, in your mercy, hear our prayer.**

Walking in this newness of life, may we always show to the world, in every aspect of our conduct, the power of the Risen Christ to heal all sin and raise up mankind to a new way of living.
**Lord, in your mercy, hear our prayer.**

Rejoicing in the new life granted us in the Easter Sacraments, we pray for all who have yet to discover, meaning and purpose in their lives, all who live in the fear of death and live without hope.
**Lord, in your mercy, hear our prayer.**

In the Easter Sacraments we have received the pledge of fullness of life in the Risen Christ. We honour the Blessed Virgin Mary to whom this fullness has been granted and ask her prayers: Hail, Mary....

In silence we ask the Spirit awaken in us a sense of our communion in the Risen Christ.

In Christ we are reconciled to the Father and have received the outpouring of the Spirit. In the power of the same spirit we cry: Our Father…

Father of life and God, not of the dead but of the living, you sent your Son to proclaim life, to snatch us from the realm of death and lead us to the resurrection. Stir up in those you have already granted a share in the life of the Risen Christ a new conviction that they have been set free from the death-dealing power of the spirit of evil and in this new conviction may they bear witness to their new life in the Risen Christ for he lives and reigns for ever and ever.

*(praying with hand outstretched over the assembly)*

Lord Jesus, by raising Lazarus from the dead you showed that you came that we might have life and have it more abundantly. By your life-giving sacraments you free us from the grasp of death and deliver us from the spirit of corruption. Through your Spirit who gives life, renew in us your gifts of faith, hope and charity that we may live with you always ever bearing witness to the glory of your resurrection for you are Lord, forever and ever. Amen

## A Blessing and a Hymn

# CHAPTER FOUR

# ENLIGHTENED

## WHAT GOD CALLS ME TO, HE EMPOWERS ME FOR

The Book of Exodus describes an event that was to begin a process of radical importance in the History of Salvation. It brought into existence the Hebrew nation, a people *defined by its covenant* with the One God of all creation. The covenant relationship was presented to them as the gift of Him who had promised their ancestor Abraham that through him all nations would be blessed. Israel's special relationship carried with it a mission: it would be the mediator between God and the rest of mankind. Through the People of God, the Lord of all creation would bring all nations back to Himself.

Some of the people who had inherited these promises saw in Jesus of Nazareth, crucified and risen, the fulfilment of them all and came to believe that the Christian community had become the people of the new and everlasting covenant promised through the prophets Jeremiah and Ezekiel. When the Liturgy offers us an invitation to renew our baptismal promises it is an invitation to renew our response to this covenant. At Easter, we celebrate the fulfilment of all God's promises but the story, now in its last age, began long ago. We can begin to reflect upon it, starting with a meeting between the

One True God and a man in his eighties. He was a shepherd, living a quiet, religious life with his wife and family and his name was Moses. God attracted his attention, and seeing that Moses 'turned aside' from all that was familiar to him, allowing himself to be drawn beyond all that he already knew, God disclosed his presence. He spoke to Moses his holy name and sent Moses to confront the most powerful man on earth. He was to require of the Pharaoh of Egypt that he free a slave population and to do so immediately. Is it any wonder that the old man said, "Who am I that I should go to Pharaoh and lead the Israelites out of Egypt?"[1]

According to the story, God championed the cause of a powerless people and appointed Moses to be the instrument of their salvation. Moses, now in his old age, had the sense to realise that he was being given a humanly impossible task. However, there had been a time when he had taken it into his head to do precisely what he was now called upon to do. Forty years before, so incensed was he by the brutality being shown his people, he had committed a murder in their defence. However, when he subsequently tried to arbitrate between quarrelling Hebrews, he was rebuffed with the challenge, "Who has appointed you ruler and judge over us? Are you thinking of killing me as you killed the Egyptian?"[2] In terror of being found out, Moses fled the country, leaving his people to their fate.

As events were to show, Moses *had not been wrong* in wanting to champion his people. In following this desire, he was actually seeking to express his authentic self – his true calling. His mistake was to try and do so in his own power. May we not say that the Lord was behind the compassion Moses felt for the people, and his ardent desire to do something to defend them? However, assuming, perhaps that this desire proceeded from his own heart, Moses took over his calling and, inevitably, had to find out that, on his own, he was as powerless as any other man to achieve his goal. It is this realisation of his weakness that made him give up. His conversion came later.

Responding with trembling to what God called him to do in his encounter with God at the burning bush, Moses came to believe two things. The liberation of his people, which he had long ago desired, was the very will of God himself. Secondly, and more importantly, he put his faith in the life-changing promise, *"I will be with you"* to accomplish the goal. He had not been on his own in his desire to do good for his people and he was now to find out that he was not alone in his powerlessness to accomplish it. According to the biblical arithmetic concerning the length of Moses' life, two thirds of it were over before he came to this life-changing realisation. He had spent forty years in Egypt, forty years as a nomadic shepherd, and he was to spend the last forty years carrying out the mission now given him.

Some of us may recognise something of our own experience in that of Moses. I grew up from infancy familiar with things 'Catholic'. I had been baptised in my infancy, confirmed and admitted to Holy Communion as a child. I had been taught, and confessed in my mind that the sacraments gave me sanctifying grace. With this cerebral knowledge, I tried to live a Christian life only to discover that I failed in all manner of ways. Like Moses in his early manhood, I had no sense of having been called by God to live the Christian life I desired to live. I saw it only as something I had decided to do. And since I saw myself as the author of the venture, I saw myself as the source of the power to achieve it. There was a dichotomy between the doctrines I professed and my actual attempts to live by what I said I believed. In other words, I knew about God's word to us in Jesus, but I was not consciously living by its power at work in me. Put another way, I knew the story of the sower who went out to sow. In primary school I had learned that this image described the work of Gospel preaching throughout the world. However, I had no realisation that this was precisely what was taking place in my own heart. What God was doing for all mankind was not more or less real than what was taking place within me. God was doing something in me which, the more I was able to assent freely to the gift, the more completely it could, in its own divine power, fulfil in me all that it had set out to do.

I was forty before I realised that not only was God the author of my desire to lead the Christian life, he was the only source of the power to live it. A false humility, which is of course another way of saying 'my pride' prevented me from realising that what God had promised everyone he ever called, from Abraham to the apostles, he promised also to me: "I will be with you." In other words, "It is in my power that you will be able to accomplish all that I have called you to be and do." In an earlier chapter, we were invited to reflect on the effects of this pride. We turn now to the belief that what God calls us to, he empowers us for.

The promise God made to Moses, he never ceased to reiterate throughout the history of salvation. Israel, called to reveal God's generous love for mankind, was also called to reveal the tragic flaw that sin has created in all mankind. It was incapable, in its own power, of keeping faith with God as the one who promised to accomplish all that he said he would do. There was a moment early on in Israel's history that was to become the archetypal moment of rebellion for all subsequent history.

The People had experienced the Lord's presence and power in their deliverance from the pursuing Egyptians; he manifested his faithful care of them in their hunger and fed them bread from heaven. Overcome by thirst, however, Israel yielded yet again to its tragic inability to trust God's promise "The place was called Massa and Meriba, because of the grumbling of the sons of Israel and because they put the Lord to the test by saying, 'Is the Lord in our midst or not?'"[3] Every day, in the Prayer of the Church, each generation is reminded not to put the Lord to this insulting test.

The Lord had introduced himself to Jacob (or Israel) as the God of his fathers Abraham and Isaac with the promise, "Know that I am with you; I will protect you wherever you go. I will never leave you until I have done what I promised you."[4] To Joshua, he promised, "I will be with you as I was with Moses; I will not leave you nor forsake you."[5] Gideon protested his powerlessness to lead Israel, "My clan is the meanest in Manasseh and I am the most insignificant in my father's house." The Lord answered, "I shall be with you."[6] Samuel "grew up and the Lord was with him not permitting any word of his to be without effect."[7] Jeremiah protested, "Ah Lord God! I know not how to speak; I am too young." But the Lord replied, "Say not, 'I am too young.' To whomever I send you, you shall go... Have no fear before them, because I am with you to deliver you."[8] The Gospel according to Matthew sees Jesus as the fulfilment of this perennial promise, proclaiming that Jesus is the Emmanuel promised by the prophet Isaiah: "Emmanuel, which means 'God is with us'."[9] And the same gospel writer gives as Jesus' final words to the apostles, "Go... and behold, I am with you always, until the end of the age."[10]

How does the Lord Jesus Christ fulfil his promise to be with us? He does so in a manner beyond all human understanding and which is the object of our faith. From his place with the Father, filled with the Holy Spirit himself, he imparts to his gathered disciples, the Holy Spirit of God. Re-examine what passed through your imagination as you read the last paragraph.

Do you imagine God being a long way off, up in Heaven, and Jesus seated at his right hand sending down the Holy Spirit? Would it not be a more accurate image to imagine Jesus the High Priest just stepping 'behind the veil' as the Letter to the Hebrews puts it?[11] The heavenly realities are not above the heavens; they are simply beyond the veil and through our union with Christ in the Spirit outpoured we are in touch with them. The image of 'touch' is clearly drawn from our physical experience and although we know we are speaking of spiritual not material realities, 'being in touch' best expresses the immediacy of the Gift of God: the Spirit outpoured.

This abiding Spirit is the source of all the gifts by which the Lord manifests his saving presence among us: it is in the power of the Spirit that God's truth is proclaimed and received, whether this is through the Scriptures or the Church's living voice. It is in the power of the Spirit that all the Sacraments are celebrated and the Church's entire worship is carried out. It is in the power of the Spirit that the whole People of God is anointed priest, prophet and king, sharing in the Lord Jesus' own christening. It is in the power of the Spirit that each person prays, "Abba, Father". It is in the power of the Spirit that the kingdom of God is established in each person's heart and they are transformed into the likeness of Christ. It is in the power of the Spirit that every form of ministry or service for the building up of the Body of Christ is carried out and bears fruit.

It may be, we once thought of ourselves as having been blessed with the teaching and example of the historical Jesus, who once lived our life on earth, and that with so generous a blessing we should be more than satisfied. This, if I may put it this way, is the blessing God offers to those he is calling to Baptism but who have not yet 'touched' the mystery.

Such knowledge is humanly accessible and through it, with God's grace working internally on the human heart, a person may come to some faith in Jesus as Lord and Saviour. This is very wonderful and it must happen to all of us. However, this is not yet the faith that enables us to recognise the immediacy of God's presence in our lives through our sacramental union with the Risen Lord Jesus. This is the faith of Christian Initiation. It is faith not only in our having been called to new life in Christ; it is faith that we are actually in communion with him and living his life in the power of the Spirit. This reality, the fulfilment of all God's promises from the beginning, "I will be with you" is totally the object of our faith. As St. Paul says, "Your life is hidden with Christ, in God."[12]

It is our faith in this hidden reality which we are invited to renew at Easter. Renewing our commitment, we shall be filled anew with the Gift of the Spirit who enables us to keep faith with our commitment. At Easter we renew the Covenant: we know, we do not have to believe, that we are willing to do our part. Living by faith, we are invited to believe and put our trust in Him who no less really, does his part.

## POINTS FOR FAITH SHARING

How seriously have I taken the idea that God calls
me to live in a personal relationship with him?
Is this something I have drawn back from,
believing myself too unworthy or unimportant
for such attention from God?

Have I assumed that things I can have a
natural knowledge about e.g. the teachings
and example of the historical Jesus, are more
real than the Spirit's gifts to me here and now?

"Pray as though everything depended on God.
Work as though everything depended on you."
(St. Augustine) This wise teaching means that
we should pray not that God might or even will
do something in answer to our prayer, but that we
should pray in the faith that he is actually doing all
that he has promised. Believing this, we get on with life,
inevitably experiencing the reality of our weakness
but putting our faith in the greater reality of his gift

Has it meant for me, in practice, 'It's nice to think God will
help but, to all intents and purposes, you are on your own.'?

## AN ACT OF WORSHIP

### A Hymn

### Opening Prayer:
Father, we come before you believing that you have called us to a blessing and a mission and that in the outpouring of your Spirit you equip us to live by the blessing and fulfil the mission. Prepare our hearts to make a radically new commitment to you when we celebrate Easter. We make our prayer etc.

### Old Testament Reading: Exodus, 3: 1-15
(Call of Moses)

### New Testament Reading: Ephesians, 1: 15-23
(The mighty power at work in us)

### Gospel: John, 20: 19-23 (Receive the Holy Spirit)

### Intercessions:
It is always possible, throughout our lives, to return if we have strayed from our first calling; it is always possible to accept our calling at a deeper level and be renewed in the grace to live out our calling. As we renew our commitment to the Lord, let us pray:
**Lord, renew in us the gifts you gave us in our Christian Initiation.**

We thank you that we are baptised. With Christ we have died to

sin and share his life with the Father, who looks upon us saying, "This is my beloved."
**Lord, renew in us the gifts you gave us in our Christian Initiation.**

We thank you that we are confirmed. Christ has breathed into us the Holy Spirit empowering us for mission. He sends us, as he was sent by the Father
**Lord, renew in us the gifts you gave us in our Christian Initiation**

We thank you that we share in the Holy Eucharist. Christ is our head, we are his members; Christ is the vine, we are the branches; Christ intercedes for all mankind and makes us sharers in this priesthood.
**Lord, renew in us the gifts you gave us in our Christian Initiation**

The Angel greeted Mary with the words, "The Lord is with you" we ask her prayers that we may respond to this greeting as she did: Hail, Mary..

Offering himself on the cross, there flowed from the side of Jesus the water and the blood, symbols of the sacraments that give life to his bride the Church. Believing in his eternal commitment to this marriage covenant, we pray: Our Father…

Father, at Easter, we recall the great events that gave us new life in Christ: the paschal mystery which we share in through our Christian Initiation. We come before you as the people you have made your own and as we pledge ourselves to serve you alone, renew in us all the gifts that will keep us faithful to so great a calling. We make our prayer through Christ our Lord.

## A Blessing and a Hymn

## THE EMPOWERING

St. Paul teaches us that, with God having redeemed mankind in the death and resurrection of Jesus, and we, having accepted this gift by faith, there is now no power in creation "able to separate us from the love of God in Christ Jesus our Lord."[13] The Lord Jesus has said of all who believe that wherever we may have wandered, we have been recalled by the Good Shepherd: "My sheep hear my voice; I know them and they follow me. I give them eternal life and they shall never perish. No one can take them out of my hand. My Father, who has given them to me, is greater than all, and no one can take them out of the Father's hand. The Father and I are one."[14] We may be grateful that the Lord enlightens our darkness about our sinful condition without him, but this enlightening will not serve its purpose unless it leads us to a profound sense of all that he calls us to and empowers us for. We do not develop simply by moving away from something; we must move towards a goal. What does God call us to? The Living Lord, the ineffable, the almighty, calls us to live in his love.

Anyone who has experienced parenthood knows how much people want to share with their children all that is in their power to give. Whatever difficulties they experienced in their own growing up, parents do not usually say to their sons and daughters, "Well, I had to pull myself up by my own bootstraps so you can jolly well do the same." The experience of most parents and children is that, while one wants adult sons and daughters to take full responsibility for their lives, parents will do all in their power to make that possible. Indeed, if their own childhood and early adult life was difficult, they usually want to make it possible that their family do not have to face the same hardships.

Preparing to renew Baptismal Promises, this experience can be the focus of prayer and reflection. As you reflect on the joys and the pains, the heartaches and the successes that love has cost you, as you reflect on the fulfilment that sharing your love with others has meant for you, the Lord will enable you to realise that he has blessed you with some inkling of what is in the Father's heart for you and for everyone. The words of Deuteronomy, although belonging to a different context, are apposite: "This command which I enjoin on you today is not too mysterious and remote for you. It is not up in the sky, that you should say, 'Who will go up in the sky to get if for us and tell us of it that we may carry it out?' Nor is it across the sea, that you should say, 'Who will cross the sea to get it for us and tell us of it, that we may carry it out?' No, it is something very near to you, already in your mouths and in your hearts. You have only to carry it out."[15] You already know from your own experience something of the love God calls us to.

It is one aspect, and surely the greatest, of our having been made in God's own image and likeness that we are capable of love. "God is love and anyone who lives in love, lives in God."[16] In recalling us to and empowering us to live in his own image and likeness, God is, above all things recalling us to love. God wants us to discover on the road to perfect love how costly it is for human beings, in whom the image and likeness of God (love) has been corrupted, to become manifestations of God's redeeming love in a sinful world. However, in lifting us out of the darkness of sin, into "his own wonderful light" that is precisely what he is doing. The cost comes in yielding to the grace that frees us of all selfishness. Mutual love's great secret is that it is utterly free. It is impossible for somebody to make us love them or for us to make another person love us. Not all the longing in the world, not all the manipulation, emotional blackmail, threats of disinheritance, punishment, nor any other created thing can command the heart of another.

If we have not turned aside from this vocation to love, but recognised it in the flesh and blood experiences of our daily lives, we are bound to have experienced the costliness of having our personal relationships purified of all the self-centredness which is another word for sin. It can be a soul-searching examination of conscience to take the words of St. Paul[17] and rewrite them to someone you say you love:

> "When by his own loving me,
> I can love you with the love that God has for you
> I shall always be patient and kind with you.
> I shall never be jealous of you or of others
> In your love of them and their love of you, etc."

Throughout our lives the One who gave us life and restored his beloved creation in Jesus Christ has been inviting us to open our hearts to the outpouring of his love, the Holy Spirit. He cannot force us to accept the Gift and for our part we have to accept the humiliating fact that, as we know in our human loves, our attachment to our own comfort can sometimes be stronger than our readiness to give ourselves to those we say we love. It is wonderful indeed, that Christ came among us that we may have life and have it to the full[18]; it is wonderful that Christ is the gate of the sheepfold and in him we may pass freely, coming and going,[19] but for people who have been institutionalised, whether by the playpen that is the law or the prison of our own selfish desires, it is a scary thing to walk out when the door is opened. We do not actually want to be all that free from some of the things we are attached to. Part of our problem as sinful people is that sin tends to blind us to just how unfree we are.

While the Church believes that we have been freed indeed from sin's reign through faith and baptism, its effects remain with us and it is by facing them in the power of God's grace that we become co-authors with God in the advancement of God's reign. The Council of Trent, stating the Catholic position on these matters called these tendencies to sin 'concupiscence'. Their existence in us should never frighten us. In the words of a charismatically gifted preacher, now deceased, "These things do not have the power to destroy you." There are words of a hymn which the author was applying to the work of spreading the Gospel throughout the world, but which we may apply to those dark places within ourselves which have yet to yield to God's saving word and be transformed by his Spirit:

> "God, whose almighty word
> Chaos and darkness heard
> And took their flight:
> Hear us, we humbly pray,
> And where the Gospel day
> Sheds not its glorious ray
> Let there be light."[20]

We have been called, then, to nothing less than a total restoration of God's work of creation. This restoration will be completed in that mystery beyond all our imagining when on the final day, God will be all in all. St. John says, "We are God's children now; what we shall be has not yet been revealed. We do know that when it is revealed we shall be like him, for we shall see him as he is."[21] In the meantime we live by faith and express our faith in the way we live our lives, a human life transformed by the love of God poured out in our hearts.

The Spirit of God is not to be found in anything that depreciates God's beloved creation. We are not angels nor have we been created to be like them. We are spiritual beings of flesh and blood and if we are ever to embody the kind of love manifested in Jesus, the embodiment of the Spirit of Love proceeding from the Father's heart, we had better not ignore our rootedness in the earth. However, we can take too much for granted that material creatures whose origins are in fixed, genetic dispositions, are capable of selfless, altruistic love.

Certainly our loving is rooted in desire and we would be sadly mistaken if we thought there was something wrong with that. Even so, this love can and does cause the lover to transcend himself. It is a wonderful thing that while desiring the presence of someone with all one's heart, a person, fired by that same love that desires the closeness of another, can be ready to lay down their life for the beloved. For love's sake, a person can suffer the absence of the beloved, even the loss that comes from their final departure. The Leonard Bernstein song, "One hand, one heart" celebrates the embodiment of, the sacrament of, divine love.

> "Make of our lives one life,
> Day after day, one life.
> Now it begins, now we start
> One hand, one heart,
> Even death won't part us now."[22]

The heart of man, as the prophet Jeremiah said, can be devious above all things, but human beings can also be very wonderful. Long before God revealed in Jesus his true image and likeness, believers, at the Spirit's prompting, looked at the mystery of mankind and without being blind to sin's effects in us, praised God in the words,

> "When I see your heavens, the work of your fingers,
> The moon and stars that you set in place –
> What are humans that you are mindful of them,
> Mere mortals that you care for them?[23]

And in another place,

> "I praise you, so wonderfully you made me;
> Wonderful are your works!
> My very self you knew;
> My bones were not hidden from you,
> When I was being made in secret,
> Fashioned as in the depths of the earth."[24]

The writer of the Letter to the Hebrews saw in psalm eight a promise of the son of man and Son of God who was to be revealed in Jesus crucified and risen, to whom is truly given "power over the works of your hands, putting all things under his feet." St. Irenaeus said, "The glory of God is man fully alive"[25] and in Jesus, crucified and risen, we see God's glory restored to creation. In Christ, God adopts us as sons and daughters, not as a legal fiction nor even by the power of a truly human love ready to treat another as one's own, but by the recreating power of his own Spirit outpoured. It is for this that he has empowered us in our Christian Initiation.

The Father says to each of us, "You are as precious to me as Jesus." At Easter we are invited to give our 'Yes' to this invitation as never before, be renewed in the Gift of the Spirit and live our lives in the life-changing realisation of who we are to God.

## POINTS FOR FAITH SHARING

As I think over my life, how have I changed
in the way I have thought God wants me to know him?

When I reflect on my capacity for sin does it lead me
to an even deeper appreciation of the depth of
God's love for me? Do I live in the realisation that
God's love is deeper than any malice I am capable of.

How do I respond to the words,
"The Father says to each of us,
"You are as precious to me as Jesus."?

# AN ACT OF WORSHIP

## A Hymn

**Opening Prayer:**
Father, in laying down his life for us, Jesus has reconciled us to you and in the outpouring of your Spirit we are recreated as your sons and daughters. May all our relationships, all our words and actions, express this, your truth about us. We make our prayer through Christ our Lord.

### Old Testament. Reading: Is. 49, 13-16.
(God's faithful love)

### New Testament Reading: 2 Cor. 13.
(the hymn to love)

### Gospel: John. 14, 15-24
(through the Spirit, the Father and the Son live in us)

**Intercessions:**
St. Augustine said of the relationship between God and us, "Deus, intimeor intimo meo": God is nearer to me than my most intimate self. Let us pray that in all we do and are, we live by this faith. We pray:
**Lord, awaken us to the reality of your presence.**

God speaks of himself as embracing us with the love of a mother for her infant. May we come to know who we are in this embrace.
**Lord, awaken us to the reality of your presence.**

The apostle reminds us that in this life we see "as in a mirror, dimly." ( I Cor. 13., 12) May the Lord renew in us his gift of faith.
**Lord, awaken us to the reality of your presence.**

Jesus speaks of us as the home in which the Father and he long to dwell. May we gladly turn aside from all that would make this impossible.
**Lord, awaken us to the reality of your presence.**

All that God's holy word reveals about each believer finds its truth in the assembly of faith which the Lord is gathering to himself. The apostles speak of us as living stones in the temple, the dwelling place of God, founded on Christ the corner stone. May we treat all brothers and sisters with the love and respect of God himself.
**Lord, awaken us to the reality of your presence.**

We honour Mary's unique role in the bringing about of God's dwelling place on earth, we ask her motherly prayer: Hail Mary…

In breathing into us his Holy Spirit, the Lord Jesus Christ shares with us his intimate life with the Father and so we pray confidently in the words he gave us: Our Father…

Father, we have no words to express our thankful praise for the mighty work of grace you are accomplishing in us. We know that it is our highest honour to be able to address you by the name given us by your only begotten Son. We know too that we pay you the highest honour by believing him and having the courage to say, "Abba"  We make our prayer etc.

## A Blessing and a Hymn

# CHAPTER FIVE

# ENTRUSTED WITH GOD'S GIFTS

Apart from the Rite of Election and the Three Scrutinies, there are two other rites which the Elect take part in during Lent. These are called the Presentations, wherein the Church, recognising in the Elect God's gift of Faith, shares with them two of its treasures: the Symbol of Faith and the Lord's Prayer. In addition there are some other rites which take place on Holy Saturday and from these we shall consider the Rite of 'Ephphatha.'

## THE PRESENTATION OF THE CREED

*"The Presentations take place after the celebration of the scrutinies. With the catechumenal formation of the elect completed, the Church lovingly entrusts to them the Creed and the Lord's Prayer, the ancient texts that have always been regarded as expressing the heart of the Church's faith and prayer. These texts are presented in order to enlighten the elect. The Creed, as it recalls the wonderful deeds of God for the salvation of the human race, suffuses the vision of the elect with the sure light of faith. The Lord's Prayer fills them with a deeper realization of the new spirit of adoption by which they will call God their Father, especially in the midst of the Eucharistic assembly."*[1]

## SYMBOLUM FIDEI – THE SYMBOL OF FAITH
### WHAT DOES IT MEAN?

A lot of the stories we learned as children came down to us across the centuries, some of them very ancient indeed. One theme retold in many tales concerned a child, usually a boy growing up in great hardship, who is discovered to be the long lost heir to a kingdom or great riches. The way the identification was made might have been a strawberry shaped birthmark, but quite often it would have been something like an ornament around the neck treasured by the child from infancy. He had never known what it meant but its true significance is revealed when it is joined to another object, and it is realised that they are two halves of a single object. The bringing together of these two halves reveals the true identity of the bearer. Such stories come perhaps from ancient pre-literary societies, or societies which were largely illiterate. Objects such as standing stones, rings or cups were invested with a meaning the culture did not have a written language to express, or which the general populace needed as a visual aid, expressing the power and authority invested in the person possessing the object.

The way the long lost heir is recognised comes from a common enough practice in the ancient world. Strangers travelling from one community to another, merchants perhaps, needed to identify themselves. The practice was to take with them a token. The token was usually part of an earthenware plate. One half was possessed by the person being visited and the other by the visitor. When the tokens fitted to each other, the authenticity of the visitor was established. In Greek, this token which guaranteed one's identity when compared with a counterpart, was called a *sumbolon*. This word was taken over into Latin as symbolum and has come down to us in English as 'symbol.'

We are probably more familiar with the meaning of a symbolum than we realise. When two people marry, they do so by making a public declaration. In our culture, signatures on a document are required by law as proof that this declaration has been made and those who witnessed the declaration have to sign it. That's the way we do things in a literate society. (There is an old Latin tag, 'Scripta manent', meaning if you just say it there is no evidence but once you write it down, it's there forever in black and white.) However, it is still the case that we regard the oral declaration by both parties as the 'wed-ding', to use an Anglo Saxon word for what is going on. Two parties make an identical declaration to each other and this act gives their union public recognition. This exchange of declarations is the symbolum of the marriage: the wedding

The ancient church has bequeathed to us such a *symbolum*. It was popularly known as Symbolum Apostolorum or Symbolum Fidei. It is known to us as The Apostles' Creed, 'creed' being derived from the first Latin word of the symbolum, 'Credo' – 'I believe'. Because of the heavy emphasis in our culture on the importance of the written word, we, perhaps, automatically think of the Creed as a *document* the ancient church handed on. It is not. It is a *recitation* or more solemnly, a *personal declaration*. In the first centuries when Christianity was not recognised in law, when it could be and was persecuted, the Symbolum Fidei was something spoken and by which believers, visiting from other cities, might be recognised. It was regarded as one of the Church's treasures, so precious that it was not committed to writing in case it be subjected to profanation and abuse by unbelievers. Only when Catechumens were judged to be sufficiently mature in their commitment, (the Elect) was it divulged to them, and then only orally. They, too, were required to commit it to memory. Even in the fourth and fifth centuries when the Church was now a public institution protected by law, one finds people like St. Ambrose, St. Augustine and St. Leo still insisting on the ancient practice of handing it on orally, and requiring that it be memorised. Christ's Church declared its faith to them and they were expected not only to consign it to memory but to 'treasure it in their hearts'.

## SHARING THE SYMBOL OF FAITH

R.C.I.A. in referring to the rite of sharing the Creed, speaks of the Church *'lovingly entrusting'* it to the Elect. When the Church shares with us a declaration of its faith, it is expressing its trust in our integrity, the genuineness of our choice to make this faith our own with a life-long commitment. The Lord Jesus Christ has said, "If you are not trustworthy with what belongs to another, who will give you what is yours?"[2] The Church makes itself answerable to the Lord in judging us worthy to be entrusted with all that the Creed offers mankind. We make ourselves answerable by accepting the trust placed in us. In imparting the

Creed to the Elect, the Church offers them a treasured possession. In receiving this gift the Elect are admitted to a company spread across the world which shares the faith it declares. The Church declares its faith to the Elect and, on Holy Saturday, before taking the final steps towards the Sacraments of Faith, they 'gave it back', declaring their life-long commitment to both this faith and the community which had shared it with them.

The Rite of Election celebrates the belief that God himself calls us to faith in Jesus Christ. In that act of worship, we celebrate the conviction that he chose us for this gift before we were born. In sharing the Creed, the People of God shares an ancient, well-guarded treasure, which honoured fore-bears have maintained for two thousand years 'in spite of dungeon, fire and sword.'[3] In doing so, the Church honours us very greatly – a pale reflection of the honour the Living God does us.

We have, no doubt, been familiar with the Creed since our childhood but as we reflect upon the Presentation of the Creed made to the Elect during the third week of Lent, and the requirement that they declare it as their own on Holy Saturday, we may be led to a new appreciation of a great gift that has long been ours.

## OURS BY GOD'S GIFT

When we were children it may be that we learned the Creed in much the same way that we learned to recite the answers to catechism questions, or any other matter our teachers handed on to us whether these were multiplication tables or irregular verbs. Indeed, it is quite possible that some of our teachers were not capable of doing any more for us than hand on information they themselves had received from others. On the other hand, most of us can remember at least one teacher, one mentor, whether in school or elsewhere who handed on to us not only information about some subject but, through their own enthusiastic love of their subject, awakened in us something deeper than a mere cerebral knowledge of what they taught. Those who devised the Creed and handed it on did so not just to pass on information. They did so in the conviction that the Creed expressed in a brief and simple way the mystery at the heart of their lives. When they declared it before one another, they were opening their hearts to one another.

We may know the Creed and be able to recite it almost without thinking, but this is not at all the same thing as realising that in these brief words, the mystery of God's grace at work in creation is being offered us to make our own. It may be that on a shelf at home we have some object of such little artistic merit or monetary value that when we die, it will be swept away in a house-clearing exercise. If our executors knew that it was the first gift given us by our first child or the last gift given by a deceased loved one, they might have more respect for it. Because we were introduced to the Creed before we became believers we may well have to learn how to appreciate what exactly has been entrusted to us. The Creed may be a commonplace thing but that does not make it any the less precious. It may be that we have in our possession something the preciousness of which we have to rediscover.

When we hear the Creed, we are hearing the voice of believers in the first centuries of the Church's history. When we make it our own, we make our own the faith they believed God was calling them to live by, and bear witness to. In joining their number we should be humbled and honoured when we remember how so many of them lost not only possessions, but health, public respect, freedom and even their lives. They knew people in their own families and their own communities who endured these things. They believed they were handing on to those who came after them a simple account of what had been made theirs through the generations of believers before them. Through their fidelity a precious gift was not lost to the world. Just as strangers presenting their half of the symbolum were saying that the token indicated their physical contact with those who had handed it over to them, so the community which shared their creed with those wishing to join them were saying that this token indicated an authentic communion with the Apostles of Jesus Christ.

Before ever it came to be known as 'the symbol of faith' and long before it came to be called 'the Apostles' Creed' it was called, 'the rule of faith', 'the rule of truth' (meaning the measure of faith and truth), 'the apostolic tradition' and "the apostolic preaching." Without access to printed Bibles such as we have, people had in a nutshell, entrusted from one generation to the next, the core of the Gospel of Christ. In possessing the Symbolum, they had a password that entitled them to take their place with every community of Christian believers in that communion of churches which spread across the known world and was called the 'Catholica'. This is that great company acknowledged in the Creed itself: the Communion of Saints. In professing the Creed, they counted themselves among that great *Gathering*, that *Assembly* or 'church' which God, in Jesus Christ was bringing into existence by the preaching of the Gospel and the outpouring of the Spirit. Owning it as an expression of the faith they had come to make their own, and proclaiming it with their voice, they were indeed claiming to be *wedded* to all believers, living and dead.

Anyone who has stood in an international assembly reciting the same creed will have experienced what an extraordinary thing it is to believe that one is visibly part of a gathering that God is bringing into existence through the preaching of the same gospel and the same response in faith. It first happened to me in the Roman Catholic Cathedral in Athens. As I looked about a congregation, which seemed to be very largely made of tourists, I saw Asians, Africans, Americans and people from all over Europe. All of us were, literally, singing from the same hymn sheets professing the same faith and celebrating our visible communion. Furthermore, I believed that beyond human vision, this very communion was with the Lord Jesus Himself whose coming into the world the Symbolum confessed, with the Spirit outpoured by the Risen Christ, and with the Father himself the Alpha and Omega, the beginning and the end of all that the Symbolum expressed.

## COMMUNION OF FAITH

The work of God's grace now revealed in Christ stretches far beyond any visible structures recognisable as pertaining to Christ's Church. In 1964, Pope Paul VI published an encyclical letter[4]. In it he gave a very fine teaching on the relationships by which all mankind is related to Christ, embodied in his Church on Earth. He had previously called the Church, as has already been mentioned, "a concrete reality penetrated by the Divine Presence." In his letter, 'Ecclesiam Suam' he was writing about the way Christ's Church could dialogue with the rest of mankind and in doing so, used the image of concentric circles. Each circle represented people's relationship to God and his revelation of himself.

The pope spoke of an outermost circle of people who seek God in nature, in their hearts, in what they see as right and wrong – in other words, mankind with no knowledge of Jesus or God's self-revealing to Israel. Further in than the outermost reaches of God's grace, he saw worshippers of the One God, living and True who has spoken through his prophets: Islam. Nearer he saw the people of the Old Covenant to whom God made promises that have never been revoked. Within the next circle, he saw all people who, holding to the scriptures of both the Old and New Testaments, profess faith in Jesus, True God and true man and who worship the One God, Father, Son and Holy Spirit. Within the inner circles, he recognised all who share the same baptism and some or all of the seven sacraments. Within the innermost circle he saw the concrete reality which is the visible, apostolic communion of all local churches in communion with the successor of Peter. In reflecting on the rite of sharing the Symbol of Faith with the Elect, realising that we have long held in our possession the confession of faith that unites us with all Christian believers, we may reflect on our own personal life of faith and our relationship to the core reality, the Risen Christ in whom our lives are hidden.

We may begin at the very centre of the concentric circles or at their fringe. If we begin at the fringe, I think of myself, born into this world utterly in the dark. I have no knowledge of myself, those who brought me into the world, the world around me or God himself. At the centre of the concentric circles, however, is the eternal God, who has from all eternity, entertained one plan for creation. Holding these two points in focus, we may begin our meditation.

However ignorant we may have been, in whatever depths of darkness we came to birth and lived our lives, nothing alters the fundamental fact: God is, and he has a purpose which involves us personally. At this point we may make our own the words of the psalmist:

> "Lord, you have probed me and you know me:
> You know when I sit and stand;
> You understand my thoughts from afar.
> My travels and my rest you mark;
> With all my ways you are familiar
> Even before a word is on my tongue,
> Lord, you know it all.
> Behind and before you encircle me
> And rest your hand upon me.
> Such knowledge is beyond me,
> Far too lofty for me to reach."[5]

In God's providence, some of us were drawn out of our total ignorance through the faith of others while we were still children. This does not need to have happened in a Christian context. We may have been taught, "The Lord is God and there is no other"[6], that we owe him our worship as our creator and our obedience because he is Lord. Who will deny that these things are true, valuable lessons for people who have to learn what is right and good? They do not lose their truth just because they are not yet the Gospel of Jesus Christ. We, however, are called beyond this point, by the Good News of Jesus, more deeply into the mystery of God's eternal plan – not just that we may live it, but that we may reveal it in our way of life and share it with others.

God's invitation to all mankind to embrace his eternal purpose was preached by the historical Jesus of Nazareth and has come down the ages even to us. In receiving as God's own word the preaching of Jesus and his apostles, as recorded in the Bible, we join the millions of people who, over two thousand years have heard it and tried to live by it. We share with them faith in Jesus as Lord, but the Catholic faith invites us to take a step in faith which some have not reached, and which they do not go beyond. They remain as listeners to the Word. They have accepted a great and holy gift of God but their worship does not lead them beyond attending with faith and devotion to this Word. We praise God for it, but it is our Catholic faith, which we share with all the Orthodox churches of the East and many heirs of the Protestant Reformation in the West that the very Word itself invites us into a sacramental reality which is nothing less than a living communion with God in Christ.

There is a real sense in which the symbolum hanging around the neck of the infant in the ancient stories, corresponds to the hidden action of divine grace in the hearts of all who, hitherto, have never encountered the Gospel of Jesus Christ. It is the task of evangelists and catechists to bring people seeking the unknown god to the realisation that the One who is drawing them in the depths of their hearts is actually drawing them into the visible communion of the Church. The gift of faith by which people come to recognise the One God, Living and True in the Gospel of Jesus Christ, is like the meeting of the two halves of the symbol. They are being called, as we ourselves have been called from the outermost fringes of the circles into the very heart of the mystery. How often has it been said by people who come to faith and the sacraments of faith, "I felt that I was coming home." God, our hidden creator calls us into the light of salvation Christ brings. In him, all find their home as he makes His home in them. Embodying this gift, they expose it in their lives, inviting the faith of others.

The Second Vatican Council spoke of the Sacred Liturgy, and the Eucharist at its centre, as the 'source and summit' of all the Church's activities. Once we have begun to understand what the R.C.I.A. is expressing about Catholic Faith, how we best apprehend it, celebrate it and live by it, we shall realise that the Holy Eucharist is indeed the very centre to which all else leads. It is as if having brought believers to the Eucharist, there is nothing beyond it but to mature more and more in what it means to be a sharer in the Sacrifice of Christ. However it is worth our considering how our childhood introduction to the Eucharist, the catechesis we received and our actual experience of taking part in the Eucharist, helped or hindered our apprehension of Catholic Faith in its fullness.

## THE SACRAMENTS ARE CELEBRATED ONLY IN THE CONTEXT OF THE WORD PROCLAIMED

Whenever we focus sharply on something, the world around it tends to slip out of focus. The more sharply we focus on the object itself, the more unconscious we become of its setting. In our childhood catechesis we were certainly given a very high appreciation of the Eucharist as the sacrament of Christ's Real Presence. But, is it possible that so sharp was the focus on this particular doctrine that we were not led to appreciate as we should the only context in which the Eucharist can exist? What is this context? It is a community of believers, attentive to the Word of God, offering God praise through a pre-existing union with Jesus Christ brought into existence by Baptism/Confirmation. Can we say we were aware of the 'summit' as something having a meaning in itself? Can we say that we had not been taught to appreciate as we should the 'mountain' of which this was the peak? Perhaps we were introduced to the summit without sufficient attention being paid to the foundations of the mountain. The 'mountain' is the whole work of evangelisation and catechesis which must underpin all experience of the sacraments.

The historical reason for the kind of catechesis we received in childhood is that we were living in a world where Catholic Doctrine was preached not so much for its own sake, but in contrast to Protestant Doctrine. Because the Protestant Reformation seemed to deny that the Mass offered us communion with Christ in the sense that the Catholic Church understood it, all catechetical emphasis was laid upon the Real Presence of Christ in the Eucharist. This was so, even though it was not until four hundred years later, that is to say, until the first half of the twentieth century, that frequent communion was restored to the laity! What is more, the Protestants, denying the reality of the Sacrament of Orders, laid stress upon the perfectly valid Catholic doctrine of the priesthood of all the baptised, conferred in Baptism. Because this was a focus of Protestant doctrine, it was down-played, or downright ignored, in Roman Catholic catechesis.

We are able to enter into, and make our own the Sacrifice of the Eucharist and the Holy Communion it makes possible, *only because* we have already made our own levels of *Com-munion* in the Body of Christ that are more radical. Whether we are going to make our Baptismal Promises at Easter or renew them, our preparation should stir up in us a profound sense of gratitude for the more radical graces we share with everyone else: our calling, our assent to the Gospel, our readiness to attend to the faith tradition of the Christian community, our choice to be a member and our election as such, our readiness to open our hearts to the purifying action of God's Holy Spirit. All these levels of communion with God himself precede our sacramental communion brought about by Baptism/Confirmation and Holy Eucharist.

In the rite we are considering today, we are invited to rejoice in a very holy and gracious gift, the foundation stone upon which all the sacraments are celebrated. The Elect, *recognised as believers in the Catholic faith*, are entrusted with the Symbol of Faith with a view to their being *enlightened* by the Spirit poured out on them in the Sacraments. In the power of the Spirit they can mature in their wonder and appreciation of all that they had been admitted to. We received the Spirit for the same purpose. Reflecting on the fact we too have been entrusted with the Church's Faith, we may pray with an expectant faith that the Spirit will open our hearts to the treasure that is now our own.

## AN ACT OF WORSHIP

### A Hymn

First Reading: Deut. 6.1-7 and psalm

Second Reading: Rom. 10.8-13

Gospel: Matt. 16: 13-18

My brothers and sisters in Christ, listen carefully to the words of that faith by which we are justified. The words are few but the mysteries they contain are great. Receive them with a sincere heart and be faithful to them.

> The Celebrant proclaims the Apostles' Creed and presents each member of the group with a copy.

> The Celebrant invites the group to proclaim the Creed

Celebrant: Let us pray that the Lord in his mercy may make us all responsive to his love revealed in the Symbol of Faith and renew in us the gifts once given us in the Baptism confessed there: forgiveness of our sins and new life in Christ.

### A time of silent prayer

Lord, we pray to you for those who profess the ancient faith of your church and accept for themselves the loving purpose and the mysteries that you revealed in the life of your Son. As they profess their belief with their lips, may they have faith in their hearts and accomplish your will in their lives. We ask this through Christ our Lord.

## A Blessing and a Hymn

## SHARING THE LORD'S PRAYER

If put to the test most of us could recite 'Old Mother Hubbard' or 'Little Boy Blue'. But how many of us know that both rhymes are believed to be veiled insults to Henry VIII's Lord Chancellor, Cardinal Wolsey. Behind the innocent lines lies a history of human passions, high politics and church history that has affected British history down to today. Many of us will recognise the lines, "Blood, toil, tears and sweat," "We shall fight on the beaches," and "This was their finest hour" as words of Sir Winston Churchill. But can we date these speeches? Can we say that we have a heart-felt appreciation of the unique and terrible prospects which Britain faced when these speeches were made? How greatly do we appreciate the consequences for this country and the world, had there not existed at that time a man whose mind and heart these words express? It is one thing to know the words; it is quite another to appreciate the extraordinary crisis in world history they refer to, and it is something else altogether to want to share the mind and heart of the person who uttered them.

We saw that handing over the Symbol of Faith is more than the ritual acceptance of a formula of words. In the creed, we were entrusted with a vision of God's gracious purpose in his creation. Those who handed on the formula of words would never have shared it with us had they not been convinced that we wanted to make this vision our own. It is the same with receiving a formula of words which Christ gave his followers. It was said that in sharing with us the Symbol of Faith and the

Lord's Prayer, Christ's Church entrusts to us two of its most precious treasures. If to accept the gift of the Symbolum is to accept the gift of the vision of God's grace in his creation, to accept from Christ this formula of words is to accept nothing less than an *entre* into the mind and heart of Him who embodies God's grace.

If possessing only the *words* leaves us, as it were, on the outside looking into the mind and heart of Jesus, we have to remember that this gift is given to the Elect with a view to their receiving the very Spirit of Adoption which enables us to enter into the mind and heart of Jesus Christ. R.C.I.A. refers to this eventuality in the words, *"The Lord's Prayer fills them with a deeper realization of the new spirit of adoption by which they will call God their Father, especially in the midst of the Eucharistic assembly."*[7] St. John Damascene said prayer is "the lifting up of the mind and heart to God"[8] and St Paul (quoting Isaiah) said, "Who has known the mind of the Lord so as to counsel him? But we have the mind of Christ."[9] The words may, in themselves, be an enlightening for the Elect, but when the Spirit is given, a new and hitherto unknown possibility is realised: the very Spirit, who guided the mind and heart of Jesus to express himself in these words, is now given to the Elect as their very own.

## THE FORMULA OF WORDS

The formula of words which we call 'The Lord's Prayer' comes down to us in two traditions, one in the Gospel according to

Matthew[10] and the other in Luke.[11] Matthew's formula has seven petitions and Luke's five. The doxology which among Protestants is added to the last petition is not regarded as scriptural but a quite late addition to the text, incorporated from the Liturgy.

In the Gospel according to Matthew, the prayer forms a part of that collection of teachings we call 'The Sermon on the Mount.' In it, Jesus teaches his followers how they should regard what have been called 'the three pillars of Jewish piety': alms-giving, prayer and fasting. Jesus says they should be carried out with a view to pleasing only the Father and not impressionable onlookers. In the Gospel according to Luke, the prayer is given on a journey from Galilee to Jerusalem. Jesus responds to his disciples' request to do for them what John the Baptist did for his disciples, "Lord, teach us to pray." It is Matthew's text that is designated 'The Lord's Prayer' and which is commonly used among all Christians. We shall look at each of the petitions that make up Matthew's version. However, before doing so, we should pause to take in the reality of an ineffable grace: we have not only been taught to pray; we have been taught by Jesus himself.

## PRAYER IN THE LIFE OF JESUS

All the Gospel narratives testify that prayer was an essential feature of Jesus' life. While this was evidently something intensely personal, something he did alone, it was not a 'hidden' activity. He wanted everyone to know it was a major feature of his life. The most superficial observation to be made on this point is that if we wish to be known as followers of Jesus but are afraid to be known as a people of prayer, we had better ask ourselves some pretty basic questions. Clearly, according to the mind of Christ, there is a great difference between giving witness to the reality of the unseen God in one's life and putting on a display of piety. Jesus speaks with disdain about using activities which are allegedly God-directed, to impress other people. What is it that so disgusts Jesus?

## THE MOST INTIMATE ASPECTS OF HIS LIFE

Of its nature, prayer must be an exposure of the innermost self to the Living God. It has to be a moment of truth. We may rightly speak of nakedness. According to the Bible, it was only when he had become a sinner that man was afraid of coming before the Lord in his nakedness. An infant has no such fear or shame with his parents and siblings. An adult has no such fear or shame in a voluntary, chosen relationship of the deepest intimacy. The man Jesus, at prayer, expresses his most real self, his personal relationship with God, and he was happy that everyone should know this. Hopefully, we too are happy for all the world to know who are the most important persons in our lives. We should be proud and happy to walk down the street coupled with someone but the relationship itself, personal and intimate, is not the object of public knowledge.

## THE INVITATION TO SHARE THE LIFE AND PRAYER OF JESUS

I, together with my sisters and brothers had a relationship to our parents. Each relationship was unique, but this uniqueness existed within the context of something shared. What we shared was ours alone: our filial relationship to a particular man and woman. Something of the same may be said of us in Christ. Our common sense tells us that Jesus has a unique relationship with the Father, something that is not ours and could never be ours. Yet we have failed to grasp the truth at the heart of the Gospel of Christ if we fail to realise that he offers us as his free gift a share in his place with the Father. We are invited to become what by nature we are not, but which by grace we can become: the children of God. What Christ is by nature, we can become by the gift of the Spirit of Adoption – the promised Gift given to us in our Christian Initiation,

In the Creed we professed that Jesus Christ is the "only begotten of the Father". We mortals have no claim on such a relationship. But Jesus came into the world "to share all that is ours that we may share all that is his".[12] This he has brought about by destroying sin and death and granting the gift of the Spirit. "He became what we are, that we might become what he is."[13] The Lord's invitation to share his way of praying is the most intimate expression of his inviting us to share his life.

In the Gospel according to John the first thing that is said to Jesus is, "Where do you live?" and he graciously said to those who did not yet know him, "Come and see." The gospel writer sees himself and us as people who are invited to know who Jesus really is: the Word made flesh and that he lives 'in the bosom of the Father'. In his invitation to "Come and see", Jesus invites us to be where he lives, to share with him as our own all that is his. When Jesus teaches us to pray, he is saying, "Pray as I do." When we pray, therefore, we are never alone. All our prayer springs from His guiding Spirit. We must learn that we are to pray in the name of Jesus Christ, that is to say, in the assurance that the Father receives the prayer of his own beloved. Look at the teaching and prayer of Jesus on the night before he died.[14] To focus consciously on these scriptural indications of what it means to make our own the Lord's way of praying, is to make our own 'The Lord's Prayer'.

## OUR FATHER, WHO ART IN HEAVEN

'Our': We never pray in isolation from Christ or our fellow members of the Body of Christ. We never come to God except in union with Christ and our fellow members of the Body of Christ. We never come to the Father except in union with the Son, as led by the Holy Spirit. Jesus came "to gather into one the dispersed children of God."[15]

'Father': The word 'Abba' is used three times in the New Testament; in the Gospel according to Mark, "Abba! Father! All things are possible to you. Take this cup away from me, but not what I will but what you will."[16]

In the Letter to the Romans: "You did not receive a spirit of slavery to fall back into fear, but you received a spirit of adoption, through which we cry, "*Abba*, Father."[17]

and in the Letter to the Galatians: "As proof that you are children, God sent the spirit of his Son into our hearts, crying out, "*Abba*, Father."[18]

'Abba' was a term of filial endearment, a very intimate and tender way of addressing one's father. It was unheard of to dare to address God so intimately. Mark puts the word on the lips of Jesus in the moment of his deepest darkness and isolation. That we are permitted even to venture into so holy a place should be a cause for the utmost reverence and silence. Paul, however, says that we who have received the Spirit of adoption are enabled to speak to God with the same intimacy.

**in Heaven:** In the world as it was imagined at the time of Jesus, one lived in one of four places: above the heavens, in the heavens, on the earth, or in the underworld. God's habitation was always imagined as beyond the heavens, that is to say, utterly unreachable to mankind. Whenever Matthew quotes Jesus speaking about or to God as 'Father', he always seems to qualify the title with such words as 'heavenly' or 'in heaven'. This seems to be his way of juxtaposing the all holiness of God with the familiarity permitted to beloved sons and daughters referred to below in the petition, 'hallowed be thy name'.

It is one of the most commonplace moments in life and yet one that brings the deepest joy when a parent hears for the first time, "Mama" or "Dada." What joy that moment must bring when someone you already know as your own recognises you, for the first time, as his own. To return for a moment to the father and infant son mentioned in Chapter Three, what a miracle of grace it would be for that father to hear his son now able to say to him, "Abba, Father." This surely lies behind the words of the Lord Jesus, "there will be more joy in heaven over one sinner who repents than over ninety-nine righteous people who have no need of repentance."[19] St. Paul hints at this mutual recognition when he compares our present life of faith with the vision that is to come: "At present I know partially; then I shall know fully, as I am fully known."[20] St. Ignatius of Antioch, at the end of a long life, bore a beautiful testimony to the enduring presence of the Spirit of adoption, long ago poured out in him. Pleading with the Christians of Rome not to obstruct his readiness to lay down his life for Christ, he said that nothing in this world held him back, "rather within me is the living water which says deep inside me: "Come to the Father."[21]

**Hallowed be thy name:** Jesus came among us so that we may become able to "worship the Father in spirit and truth."[22] Perhaps one aspect of this mystery is for us humans to hold in balance both intimacy and respect. Mankind must ever hold in awe the utter holiness of God, a truth expressed in the Second of the Ten Commandments, and fear of the Lord or, awe in his presence, is the beginning of wisdom.[23] Both Mark and Paul couple the two words, 'Abba' and 'Father', the intimate with the formal, perhaps to remind us that the gift of intimacy with God must ever be rooted in awe. If indeed, awe in the presence of God is the beginning of wisdom, if this is where true discipleship begins, Paul reminds us that faith enables us to recognise in Christ, "the power of God and the wisdom of God".[24] We who make our approach to God through Jesus must ground our approach in awe at so great a grace.

**Thy Kingdom come:** God's reign will be fully realised when "Christ hands over the kingdom to his God and Father" and God is "all in all".[25] The first Christians prayed earnestly for that eventuality: "The one who gives this testimony says, "Yes, I am coming soon." Amen! Come, Lord Jesus!"[26] Maranatha! How can anyone read those final words of the New Testament without sharing the intensity of their longing? It is always a joy to share in that canticle, sung in the Church's Evening Prayer on Thursdays, "We give thanks to you, Lord God Almighty, who is and who was, because you have taken your great power and have begun to rule".[27] While we may be privileged to share in the prayer of the first Christians awaiting that cosmic event, we have to remember that God must first reign in our hearts. Every aspect of our human being must be integrated into the Reign of God. We must pray just as earnestly for this eventuality.

**Thy will be done, on earth as it is in heaven:** The will of God, eternally existing "in heaven" is that "everyone be saved and come to knowledge of the truth."[28] This eternal purpose is now revealed and accomplished in the Crucified and Risen Lord Jesus. God's Holy Church, the Body of Christ on earth, is a sacrament and instrument of the reconciliation brought about in Christ. Its worship mirrors the heavenly liturgy carried out by Christ our High Priest in the heavenly places. In the same way, the bonds of love and reconciliation that exist among its members on earth must mirror the harmony of heaven. The Book of Acts[29] offers an idealised description of the church on earth. It should be our constant prayer that the honour of God's holy name, associated with all the Church's activities, be not compromised by what people see in the Church.

**Give us this day our daily bread:** In the Gospel according to Matthew, the Lord's Prayer is presented after a warning from the Lord about the way those who bear his name pray, and is followed by a warning of being preoccupied with future cares. They are not to pray like pagans. What does Jesus mean by this? People who are not sure who God is, what he is like, whether he actually exists or is remotely interested in our prayers, 'babble'. They do not know who it is to whom they speak, and so their 'prayer' expresses their uncertainty and helplessness. Those who call themselves followers of Jesus must be converted from this ignorance so that their prayer springs from a full confidence in the Father of our Lord Jesus Christ. Prayer that is a shot in the dark rather than an expression of one's confidence in a father's love is not Christian prayer. This petition expresses confidence in 'Abba' who knows our needs before we ask him.

**And forgive us our trespasses as we forgive those who trespass against us:** Earlier on in the Sermon on the Mount, Jesus warns his followers not to adopt a narrow interpretation of the commandments such as that taught by the Scribes and Pharisees, but to be open hearted: "perfect, just as your heavenly Father is perfect."[30] If our relationship with God is truly grounded in the faith that we are reconciled to him by his free gift in Jesus Christ, it is impossible for us to harbour an unforgiving heart. We may rejoice to believe that God in Christ restores us to his image and likeness, but our readiness to make this petition is the acid test of whether or not we really want this to happen.

In this matter, Christians must not confuse feelings that arise from injury and insult with a wilful resistance to forgiving others. If we have been insulted and injured by someone, all the forgiveness in the world is not going to free us from the hurt we have experienced at the hand of another. It is only when we own the pain we are undergoing, that we can come to a clear choice about how to react to the person who caused the pain. The forgiveness God offers us in Christ is not based on a pretence that there is really nothing to forgive; to own the injury and in the face of it to forgive is to embody divine forgiveness.

**And lead us not into temptation:** The English verb used here translates a Greek verb meaning 'do not allow us to' or 'do not let us yield to'.

"No one experiencing temptation should say, 'I am being tempted by God'; for God is not subject to temptation to evil and he himself tempts no one. Rather, each person is tempted when he is lured and enticed by his own desire."[31]

"No trial has come to you but what is human. God is faithful and will not let you be tried beyond your strength; but with the trial he will also provide a way out, so that you may be able to bear it."[32]

"Since we have a great high priest who has passed through the heavens, Jesus, the Son of God, let us hold fast to our confession. For we do not have a high priest who is unable to sympathize with our weaknesses but one who has similarly been tested in every way, yet without sin. So let us confidently approach the throne of grace to receive mercy and to find grace for timely help."[33]

It is easy for Christians to forget, especially when under stress, that the very Spirit with which Jesus was made able to face temptation has been given to all of us in our Christian Initiation. At the beginning and at the end of his public life, Jesus confronted and overcame temptation by prayer; in the power of the Spirit, we can do the same.

**But deliver us from evil:** Through our Christian Initiation we are taken up into Christ's victory over all sin and death, "delivered from the power of darkness".[34] When I was a seminarian in my early twenties we used to smile, with the shallowness of youth, at the advice with which our confessor invariably ended each confession, "Keep persevering." Now in old age, I smile at the soundness of the advice. Experience teaches us the profound need to 'pray without ceasing'[35] in the conviction that no "creature will be able to separate us from the love of God in Christ Jesus our Lord."[36]

## AN ACT OF WORSHIP

### A Hymn

### A Liturgy of the Word (Lectionary Vol.III, p.10-13)

First Reading: Hosea 11: 1b, 3-4, 8c-9, with psalm

Second Reading: Rom. 8: 14-17, 26-27

Celebrant: Let us stand to receive the words in which our Lord teaches his followers to pray: Matt. 6, 9-13

Celebrant: Let us pray: In the waters of baptism we received the forgiveness of our sins and the outpouring of the Spirit of adoption. May the Lord open our hearts to the wonder of all that we have received.

### A time of silent prayer

### All recite together the Lord's Prayer

Father we stand before you as your own sons and daughters, called and chosen by you live to live in this grace and bear witness of it to others. May the gracious words your beloved Son has taught us and which we take on our lips rise up from hearts anointed in the Spirit and find daily expression in the lives we live. We ask this through Christ our Lord.

### A Blessing and a Hymn

## THE 'EPHPHATHA'

This rite is not presented in R.C.I.A. as the most important. Indeed, it is quite possibly omitted by some. It is the last of the acts of worship celebrated with the Elect before their actual Christian Initiation. It takes place on Holy Saturday while they are preparing themselves for that event by observing the Paschal Fast.

In this reflection on the rite, the Gospel narrative on which the rite is based is associated with words taken from the Prophet Isaiah. This connection is not to be found in the books of the Sacred Liturgy. It is hoped that prayerful reflection on what is said here will open minds and hearts to the wonderful work of grace a well-prepared for Christian Initiation is supposed to effect.

## AN OPEN HEART

Ava Gardner, the beautiful Hollywood star of yester-year is reported to have said, "Deep down I am a very shallow person." although I have also read that her words were, "Deep down I am pretty superficial."[37] The Bible has a word for this deep down part of us, the inner person or, as we might say nowadays, 'the real me'. The word is 'heart'. It is a word that occurs hundreds of times throughout the Bible.

*"The Lord said to Samuel: 'Do not judge from his appearance or from his lofty stature, because I have rejected him. Not as man sees does God*

*see, because man sees the appearance but the Lord looks into the heart."*[38] The Lord knows us better than we know ourselves and we must accept with courageous faith that he knows who it is he has called and chosen.

*"More tortuous than all else is the human heart, beyond remedy; who can understand it? I, the Lord, alone probe the mind and test the heart."*[39] The prayers made in the Scrutinies were offered, that we might let the Holy Spirit bring to consciousness those areas in our heart where we most need God's healing grace – painful, but the step that leads to freedom.

*"A clean heart create for me, God; renew in me a steadfast spirit."*[40] This psalm just has to be the most appropriate prayer for Lent. It is truly the word of God assuring us that real repentance leads to nothing less than a new creation.

*"I will give them a new heart and put a new spirit within them; I will remove the stony heart from their bodies, and replace it with a natural heart."*[41] The new heart is not brought about by our action or effort; it is an act of God – a new creation. However, true repentance which is itself the effect of God's guiding hand on us, must precede it.

It is the Spirit who will effect this transformation of us, restoring 'the real me,' "may he grant you to be strengthened with power through his Spirit in the inner self … that Christ may dwell in your hearts through faith."[42] It is the Promised Gift given in the Sacraments of Christian Initiation who, by the time we enter heaven, will have transformed us into the image and likeness of God. The purpose of Lenten purification and enlightenment is to bring us to the point where we open this deep heart, unafraid because of our unlikeness to God, entrusting ourselves to all that God promises. The Exodus, the passage from slavery to freedom which the Hebrews made under Moses' leadership, was a divine action by which the People of God were formed. The Passover accomplished by the Lord Jesus Christ in his journey through death to eternal life, is the real Exodus. On Easter Night all who have heard his call are led by him into the water of baptism and, under his leadership, make this journey to freedom from the yoke of sin. The Promised Land to which he leads his people is new life with God, the reign of God brought about by the outpouring of the Spirit. By this gift, God begins to reign in our hearts.

The Church's faith on this point is clearly expressed in the prayer that is made after the third reading in the Easter Vigil: "Father, even today we see the wonders of the miracles you worked long ago. You once saved a single nation from slavery and now you offer that salvation to all through baptism. May the peoples of the world become true sons of Abraham and prove worthy of the heritage of Israel." An alternative prayer makes precisely the same point: "Lord God, in the new covenant you shed light on the miracles you worked in ancient times: the Red Sea is a symbol of our baptism and the nation you freed from slavery is a sign of your Christian people. May every nation share the faith and privilege of Israel and come to new birth in the Holy Spirit."[43]

If these prayers evoke in us a wonder at the miracle of compassionate grace shown us in our call to Baptism, we easily realise why the call to this grace began with the words, "Repent and believe." The tragedy of the first Exodus is that this did not happen. Indeed, Moses' leadership did not have the power to bring about this new creation of the inner person. The first Exodus pointed the way to the real leadership of Jesus crucified and risen. Indeed the very accounts of Israel's call to freedom recall with bitter sadness that there was something that prevented them from reaching the Promised Land. It is a condition that throughout the Bible is called 'hardness of heart'. Psalm 78 (77 in the Vulgate) describes this radical obstacle to God's grace. The Letter to the Hebrews, Chapters 3-5, warns us not to let happen to us what happened to the people of the first Exodus. Every single day in the Church's Prayer, one of the first things we do is recite Psalm 95: "Oh that today you would listen to his voice: harden not your hearts."

The psalmists, among many other Old Testament witnesses, testify against the People of God for choosing this response throughout their entire history. We do wrong if we imagine that the Old Testament points a finger at Israel as being responsible for something the rest of mankind was not also involved in! In the same way that the Law revealed the nature of sin without having the power to do anything about it, so the history of the People of God reveals that mankind does not have it in its power to save itself. It needs the grace of God which changes the heart.

## MANKIND'S HARDNESS OF HEART

When the eyes and ears of the priest Isaiah were opened to the ineffable grace of God's presence in Israel, and the unawareness in which he and the rest of the nation lived, he offered to carry the Word of God to his people. The Lord's response was expressed in perhaps the most chilling words of the Bible. God says, in effect, "You can do what you will but remember you are banging your head against a brick wall." Mankind is set on a path that, left to his own devices, can lead to nothing more than ever greater deafness and complete blindness. The arteries are hardening and there is no power in the world to stop total sclerosis.[44] Rightly or wrongly, it appears to me that this is the only Old Testament text which Matthew, Mark, Luke and John quote.

When I was a child in primary school, teachers told me that Jesus of Nazareth, a master of story-telling, chose images from the everyday life of his listeners to speak of the Kingdom of God. This may well be the case. However, immediately accessible as these images may have been, the Lord Jesus gave an entirely different reason for speaking about the mystery of God's Reign in this way. He said, in effect, that people will hear only what they want to hear and so their minds and hearts are closed to what he is offering them.

**Matthew 13, 14-15:** "The reason I talk to them in parables is that they look without seeing and listen without hearing or understanding. In their case this prophecy of Isaiah is being fulfilled."

**Mark 4. 12:** "When alone with the disciples, they ask Jesus what the parables meant: "The secret of the kingdom of God is given to you but to those who are outside everything comes in parables so that (in this way the prophecy is fulfilled.)"

**Luke 8. 10:** "His disciples ask him what this parable might mean and he said, "The mysteries of the kingdom of God are revealed to you; for the rest there are only parables so that 'they may see but not perceive, listen but not understand'."

In the case of John and Acts, the text is used to express an almost overwhelming sense of tragedy that people are unable and unwilling to be led beyond what, in the narrowness of their heart's vision, they imagine is possible or desirable.

**John 12. 40:** "Though they had been present when he gave so many signs they did not believe in him; this was to fulfil the words of the prophet Isaiah: "Lord who could believe what we have heard said and to whom has the power of the Lord been revealed[45] Indeed, they were unable to believe because, as Isaiah says again, "He has blinded their eyes, he has hardened their heart, for fear they should see with their eyes and understand with their heart and turn to me for healing."[46]

**Acts 28. 26-27:** Paul makes contact with the Jews of Rome and spends all day trying to convince them that Jesus is the fulfilment of the Law and the Prophets, "some were convinced by what he said while the rest were sceptical. So they disagreed among themselves, and as they went away Paul had one last thing to say to them, 'How aptly the Holy Spirit spoke when he told your ancestors through the prophet Isaiah; "Go to this nation and say…." Understand then, that this salvation of God has been sent to the pagans; they will listen to it'."

The image which this dreadful vision presents to my imagination is that of a door firmly locked. Yet, according to the Letter to the church in Leodicea,[47] Jesus says, "Behold, I stand at the door and knock. If anyone hears my voice and opens the door, I will enter his house and dine with him and he with me." To whom are these most gracious words uttered? They offer heart felt conversion to people described in the very same letter, "as neither hot nor cold". So utterly indifferent to the Word of God are they that he who admonishes them says, "I will spit you out of my mouth." The conjunction of these two images, the Lord's disgust, and at the same time his readiness to come if welcomed, should alert us to any projecting onto God of the hardness of heart the Sacred Scripture denounces in mankind! The words spoken to Isaiah describe not a reluctance in God to do something about mankind's hopeless situation, but the need for that divine intervention which alone can set matters right. We call this intervention, God's grace.

It has been said earlier on, that if we are ever to be in a position to embrace the revelation of God's grace to mankind in Christ, we must believe him when he says that mankind is terminally sick. Although this sickness exists in us more deeply than our power to choose, such choices as we make, unguided by God's grace, simply lead us more deeply into its grip. The rite of

'Ephphatha' takes place after a long process of conversion. The process is not one of self-help, but a process of yielding more and more to the gift of faith which enables us to stand before our Saviour with nothing but faith in his power and readiness to save us. The 'Ephphatha' is a joyful celebration of the grace to which the Catechumens have responded. When the Church performs the action of our Saviour, it proclaims the blessing that breaks the dreadful curse. It is, indeed, a concrete reality penetrated by the divine presence.

The process of our conversion begins with our being exposed to the Gospel of Christ. Whether this happens to us through those who brought us up, or whether we came to some knowledge of Jesus in later life, is not the issue. One way or another, at some point in our lives, we have to make a choice. Do I or do I not believe that in very ordinary human events in my perfectly ordinary life, God has been calling me? The God of Abraham, Isaac and Jacob, the God of Moses and Elijah, the God who became man in the person of Jesus Christ has actually been calling me. He has been calling me, to use words many of us have known since childhood, "to know him, love him and serve him in this life and to be happy with him in the next."

If we realise that this is indeed so, we are bound to ask, "What must I do" as did those who were "cut to the heart" by the words of Peter on the day of Pentecost. "You must repent and every one of you must be baptised in the name of Jesus Christ for the forgiveness of your sins and you will receive the gift of the Holy Spirit. The promise that was made is for you and your children and for all those who are far away, for all those whom the Lord our God will call to himself."[48]

When someone commits his life to Jesus Christ with a view to being baptised in his name, he does so in the conviction that God has first made a commitment to him: through Jesus Christ, the Lord God will fulfil every promise he ever made. The entire Catechumenate was meant to bring us to the point where we are prepared to 'take the plunge' in the waters of Baptism, and find out through the outpouring of the Spirit what God has wanted to share with us. God has successfully broken through all the crust of our sins and enabled us to receive his grace in our innermost hearts. As we pass with Jesus through the waters, in the conviction that he is leading us into a new way of living, that is to say, as he leads into the new life he now lives with God, we shall discover the Lord has indeed, taken away our heart of stone, releasing the Spirit, the ever gushing fountain of life which can now leap up in our own deepest hearts.

The Promised Gift given in our Christian Initiation, the Holy Spirit of God, is given us not only that we may hear the Word of God and live by it, but that we may gladly proclaim that word, bearing witness to all that God has graciously done for us. In the rite of 'Ephphatha' the Church makes the prayer, in the name and power of Jesus, that He who has guided our steps thus far in the pilgrimage of faith, will remove all obstacles to our hearing the Word who effects so great a change in us. The 'Ephphatha' prayer is made that we may open wide our hearts, welcoming the Spirit into our deepest selves. Inspired by the

Spirit may our tongues be loosened so that we burst into grateful praise in a way that bears witness to his holy name. The Book of Revelation describes the Elect celebrating God's victory by singing, "the song of Moses, the servant of God and the song of the Lamb."[49] On Easter Night the whole People of God, washed clean in the blood of the Lamb, make their own the song of Moses and all Israel, "I will sing to the Lord, glorious his triumph!"[50]

The man who was unable to hear and unable to communicate, symbolises an inability to hear, to take to heart, God's saving word. Freeing him from this disability, the Lord gives him the readiness and the power to speak boldly about what the Lord has done in his life. The effect of the Lord's act of mercy, and the man's testifying to it, is that it creates 'unbounded admiration' for the Lord. Can we recognise ourselves and our calling in this sign? Let us pray for each other and for the group as a whole, if indeed a parish group is using this text in its preparation for Easter, the prayer mentioned earlier from the Letter to the Ephesians:

"I kneel before the Father, from whom every family in heaven and on earth is named, that he may grant you in accord with the riches of his glory to be strengthened with power through his Spirit in the inner self, and that Christ may dwell in your hearts through faith; that you, rooted and grounded in love, may have strength to comprehend with all the holy ones what is the breadth and length and height and depth, and to know the love of Christ that surpasses knowledge, so that you may be filled with all the fullness of God. Now to him who is able to accomplish far more than all we can ask or imagine, by the power at work within us, to him be glory in the church and in Christ Jesus to all generations, forever and ever. Amen."[51]

## AN ACT OF WORSHIP

A Hymn

First Reading: Isaiah, 6, 8-10

Psalm: 95 (V. 94)

Gospel: Mark, 7, 33-37

The Celebrant approaches each person
signing the ears and the lips
with a sign of the cross, saying:

Ephphatha: that is, be opened,
that you may profess the faith you hear
to the praise and glory of God

A Blessing and a Hymn

## CHAPTER SIX

# INITIATED INTO CHRIST'S CHURCH

### HOLY BAPTISM

These reflections began with R.C.I.A.'s distinction between an adequate awareness of Christian Doctrine, and a profound sense of the Christian Mystery. To acquire this sense, it was said, prepares the heart more than anything else to receive the grace of God offered in the Sacraments of Christian Initiation: Baptism, Confirmation and Holy Eucharist. These reflections have been offered so that during Lent, purified by the Holy Spirit and enlightened by his gift, people who are to renew baptismal promises will do so with the same fervour and sincerity that is expected of the catechumens in making them. As a consequence, having renewed their commitment to the Lord Jesus with expectant faith, they may be blessed with a new outpouring of the Spirit such as the catechumens may rightly look for.

The Easter Vigil, at the heart of the Easter Triduum of the Lord's Death and Resurrection, celebrates the source of the Church's life: the forgiveness of sins and the new life in the Spirit. It is for this reason that it in the midst of this celebration new members of the Body of Christ are brought to birth in the waters of the font, anointed with the Spirit, and take their place in the Eucharist, 'the source and summit' of all the Church's activities. As the Sacred

Liturgy of Lent moves towards the Paschal Triduum, a series of images is put before the Sunday assemblies of Catechumens and Faithful. While they were chosen initially with Catechumens in mind, they are intended to lead everyone into a deep appreciation of what it means to be made sharers in Christ's Paschal Mystery through the Sacraments of Christian Initiation.

## SON OF MAN

On the first Sunday of Lent, the Christian Assembly is presented with the image of the man who is like us in all things but sin. In the Gospel according to Mark, he is first presented to us as one of the crowd, one man among many, a man among sinners drawn by the preaching of John the Baptist. However, while in obedience to God's prophet he took his place before him with the rest of mankind, he was singled out by the voice of God, "You are my beloved Son; with you I am well pleased."[1] As the forty days of purification and enlightenment begins, the Assembly is invited to contemplate this Jesus, driven by the very Spirit of God to face the full onslaught of temptation. This is the temptation we all have to face. We have to choose between yielding to the temptation to create for ourselves a purpose in life without regard for God or man, or willingly embrace that purpose for which God lovingly called us out of nothing and gave us life.

St. Augustine invites us to consider the wonderful grace that is given us by being initiated into the Christian Mystery. "If in

Christ we have been tempted, *in him* we overcome the devil. Do you think only of Christ's temptations and fail to think of his victory? See yourself as tempted in him and see yourself as victorious in him. He could have kept the devil from himself but if he were not tempted he could not teach you how to triumph over temptation."[2] At the end of Lent, we are to see Jesus once again facing the full onslaught of evil and defeating it in the power of God. Indeed, we see him so utterly overcoming all evil that he is victorious over even death itself. At Easter, we shall worship him as God's champion, ready to lead all mankind out of darkness into the kingdom of God. This is the Good News we have been called to hear. Do we, as St. Augustine asks, recognise who we are in the Risen Christ? The very Spirit of God who led Jesus through temptation and death to the fulfilment of God's purpose for all mankind is the Spirit we receive in our Christian Initiation.

## SON OF GOD

In contrast to the humble image of Jesus enduring temptation, there is put before us on the Second Sunday of Lent an awe-inspiring image of Jesus the Christ. We see the carpenter from Nazareth transfigured by the glory of God.

This same man, one of us, is in conversation with the pillars of the Old Covenant, Moses and Elijah, the very embodiment of Law and Prophecy, and according to Luke, they are talking about his Passover which he is to accomplish in Jerusalem. Furthermore he is over-shadowed by the very Cloud of God's

Presence. This is the sign that the Lord gave Israel that he was indeed with his people. It is the pillar of cloud that accompanied them in the desert and the cloud that filled the Temple at its dedication, the 'Shekinah'. The God who had made the Covenant says of Jesus, "This is my beloved. Listen to him." Those who did listen and have passed on to us their testimony, present Jesus as the fulfilment of all that the Old Covenant promised. Indeed, they present his dying and rising as the fulfilment of the Passover itself, the act of worship in which each generation of Israel defined itself as heirs of the Covenant. These witnesses of Jesus give us his words on the night he began to accomplish his Passover, and gave us the gift by which we celebrate our sharing in it, "This cup is *the new covenant* in my blood. Do this, as often as you drink it, in remembrance of me."[3]

Jesus gave his companions the experience of his transfiguration and the testimony of the Old Testament to strengthen them for the coming scandal of the cross. However, St. Leo the Great teaches us that he had another purpose. "With no less forethought he was also providing a firm foundation for the hope of holy Church. The whole body of Christ was to understand the kind of transformation that it would receive as his gift. The members of that body were to look forward to a share in that glory which first blazed out in Christ the Head."[4] It is in the Sacraments of Christian Initiation that we are made members of the Body of Christ, coheirs with Christ.

Having been confronted with these two contrasting icons of Jesus Christ, the Assembly is presented on the following three

Sundays of Lent with three invitations to faith in Jesus as our Saviour. These are three of the signs Jesus gave, according to the Gospel of John: Jesus' invitation to the Samaritan woman, his healing of the man born blind and his raising Lazarus from the tomb.

## WATER AND THE SPIRIT

St. Augustine invites us to see in the Samaritan woman, "a symbol of the Church not yet made righteous but about to be made righteous. Righteousness follows from the conversation. She came in ignorance; she found Christ and he enters into conversation with her." Throughout the Catechumenate those being called to Baptism have been in dialogue with the one calling them. The same is true of us, if we take seriously the call to be renewed in all that Baptism offered us. St. Augustine invites us to "recognise ourselves in her words and in her person and with her give our own thanks to God."[5] She had come to draw water and finding faith in Jesus she is a symbol of what was to come, "If you knew the gift of God and who is saying to you, "Give me a drink" you would have asked him and he would have given you living water."[6]

The entire thrust of the Catechumenate is to bring new believers to a profound sense of the as yet unknown gift that is to be given in the waters of Baptism. "The water I give him will become in him a spring of water welling up to eternal life."[7] In another place Jesus said, "Whoever believes in me, as scripture says, 'Rivers of living water will flow from within him'." The Gospel writer's comment on this promise is, "He said this in reference to the Spirit that those who came to believe in him were to receive. There was, of course, no Spirit yet, because Jesus had not yet been glorified."[8] As people who have already received this Gift, we wish to open our hearts more deeply to this outpouring of the Spirit by making a new commitment to the giver of the Gift.

## ENLIGHTENED BY THE LIGHT OF THE WORLD

On the fourth Sunday of Lent, we see Jesus sending a man born in darkness to the pool that will bring him healing.[9] The evangelist says that the name of this pool, 'Siloam' means 'sent'. Those preparing for Baptism and those already baptised are invited to see in the life-changing act of Jesus for this man, his life-changing action in our lives. Christ offers a radical healing and sends us as witnesses to those who have yet to receive this blessing.

"We are of Adam's stock," says St. Augustine. "Blind from our birth; we need him to give us light."[10] A number of commentators see in the fact that Jesus took up earth and making mud of it plastered it on the man's sightless eyes, a completion of God's action described in Genesis: taking mud and forming man from it into his own image and likeness.[11]

The healing Christ offers us reaches to the roots of our creation. As one of the prayers following the proclamation of Creation at the Easter Vigil says, "You created all things in wonderful beauty and order. Help us now to perceive how still more wonderful is the new creation by which in the fullness of time you redeemed your people through the sacrifice of our Passover, Jesus Christ."[12]

The Liturgy invites the Catechumens, and us, to see in Jesus the one who successfully confronts sin, and every other obstacle to our achieving the purpose for which God created us. We may be sure that in accepting his invitation to follow him into the Paschal Mystery we shall share the restored glory it brings. In doing so we shall be enlightened, discovering that he is indeed "the light of the world" and who ever follows him "will not walk in darkness." From ancient times Baptism has been called 'Enlightenment.' If we really want to be renewed in all that our Christian Initiation gave us, we can do no better than pray that the Lord will remove the scales from our eyes so that we may come alive with a new perception of all that has been done for us; we are indeed, on the right path. The Lord has been with us throughout the history of our calling, guiding our steps to this moment of choice. There can be no doubt that in the power of this new illumination, we shall be inspired by the same gratitude which prompted the once-blind man to testify to Jesus before all the world.

## PASSAGE FROM DEATH TO NEW LIFE

The story of Lazarus put before us on the Fifth Sunday of Lent challenges the faith of the Catechumens and ours to its depths. In short, there is little point in our celebrating Easter if we do not believe that through the Easter Sacraments, we too already share what happened to the man, Jesus of Nazareth, in his Passover.

"Are you unaware that we who were baptised into Christ Jesus were baptised into his death? We were indeed buried with him through baptism into death, so that, just as Christ was raised from the dead by the glory of the Father, we too might live in newness of life. For if we have grown into union with him through a death like his, we shall also be united with him in the resurrection. We know that our old self was crucified with him, so that our sinful body might be done away with, that we might no longer be in slavery to sin. For a dead person has been absolved from sin."[13]

Addressing the newly baptised, the famous Jerusalem Catechesis of the fifth century says: "Solomon's phrase in another context is very apposite here. He spoke of *a time to give birth and a time to die*. For you, however, it was the reverse: a time to die, and a time to be born, although in fact both events took place at the same time and your birth was simultaneous with your death.

"This is something amazing and unheard of! It was not we who actually died, were buried and rose again. We did these things only symbolically but we have been saved in actual fact. It was Christ who was crucified, who was buried and who rose again, and all this has been attributed to us. We share in his sufferings symbolically and gain salvation in reality. What boundless love for men! Christ's undefiled hands were pierced by the nails; he suffered the pain. I experience no pain, no anguish, yet by the share that I have in his sufferings he freely grants me salvation."[14]

In our Christian Initiation, we have been recreated and now live in Christ with God. We know that this life is the object of our faith not the object of our feelings or rational analysis. However, "we are God's children now; what we shall be has not yet been revealed. We do know that when it is revealed we shall be like him, for we shall see him as he is."[15] We shall certainly die in the flesh, but we shall die in Christ, already alive in him by the outpouring of the Spirit given us in Baptism. The Lord Jesus assures us as he assured Martha, "I am the resurrection and the life; whoever believes in me, even if he dies, will live and everyone who lives and believes in me will never die."[16]

That we may take to heart the full impact of these words the Lord spoke to Martha, we have to remember that Jesus did not introduce her to the hope of resurrection. As her own words make clear, she entertained a hope of resurrection on the last day, before she knew Jesus. He had not given her that hope; she had received it in her upbringing. The utterly new and radically challenging word of Jesus is that HE is the hope that God had awakened in Israel and in her, "I am the resurrection."

All mankind walks on a downward path, a journey that leads only to death. Our vocation to the Gospel and the Sacraments of faith is an invitation to turn aside and hear a voice that says, "I am the way, and the truth and the life."[17] St. Paul, quoting Deuteronomy says, " 'The word is near you, in your mouth and in your heart,' (that is, the word of faith we preach) for if you confess with your mouth that Jesus is Lord, and believe in your heart that God raised him from the dead, you will be saved."[18]

## "HEAVEN IN ORDINARIE"[19]

These words of the poet George Herbert, call to my mind an expression used in the Gospels at the end of the Transfiguration experience. The chosen witnesses looked and saw "only Jesus." This phrase has always suggested to me the 'ordinary,' the presence of someone who had become for these men, their everyday experience. In the transfiguration, a vision had been granted them that they might see with faith beyond their ordinary and everyday assessment of reality and recognise, in the man Jesus, a concrete reality penetrated by the Divine Presence: Christ the Lord.

The preaching of the Holy Gospel and our formation in the tradition of the Church, (evangelisation and catechesis) has brought us to the Mystery of Faith. This is Christ, Head and members, the Body of Christ on earth, his Church, his Gathering, his Assembly. This is the concrete reality penetrated by the Divine Presence into which we are invited to come. However, we see and hear with our bodily senses only the ordinary, the everyday, the human. By God's gift of faith, we recognise God's Christ. The Christian Mystery is "Christ among you your hope of glory."

The Catechumens, who have listened to the Word, taken it to heart and resolved to dedicate their lives to Jesus, stand at the threshold of this Mystery. Only by God's action can they enter. They enter and become sharers in the Mystery by the "concrete realities penetrated by the Divine Presence", which we call the Sacraments of Christian Initiation: Baptism, Confirmation and Holy Eucharist. All of us, baptised in infancy, have received this initiation; it is unrepeatable. Even so, we can spend the days of Lent yielding to the enlightenment and purification the Spirit offers us, and make a radically new dedication of our lives to Jesus. In doing so, we may confidently look forward to a new outpouring of the Gift in whose power we can live the Christian Mystery, and bring the good news of it to others.

## SACRED CHRISM

At Mass in the Cathedral on the morning of Maundy Thursday you will have witnessed the solemnity with which the oil of Chrism is blessed. The blessing of oil of catechumens and the oil of the sick each have their own dignity, but the invocation of the Holy Spirit on the oil mixed with perfumes which is to be used in the sacrament of Confirmation is different. It is carried out with the same solemnity as the invocation of the Holy Spirit at Mass. The bishop and all the concelebrating clergy extend their hands in blessing. In calling the Holy Spirit upon this oil the bishop prays that those who will be anointed with it will be granted "royal, priestly and prophetic honour."[20] In the fifth century Jerusalem Catechesis, we can sense the high reverence in which sacred chrism was held.

Commenting on the psalm, "God, your God, has anointed you with the oil of gladness above all your fellows," it tells the newly-baptised, "The oil of gladness with which Christ was anointed was a spiritual oil; it was in fact the Holy Spirit himself who is called the oil of gladness because he is the source of spiritual joy. But we too have been anointed with oil, and by this anointing we have entered into fellowship with Christ and have received a share in his life. Beware of thinking that this holy oil is simply ordinary oil and nothing else. After the invocation of the Spirit it is no longer ordinary oil but the gift of Christ and by the presence of his divinity it became the instrument through which we receive the Holy Spirit."[21] I imagine we are still familiar with the notion that oil suggests athletic strength, but St. John Chrysostom adds that the perfume evokes an image of a bride.

In the Letter to the Hebrews, written between AD 60 and 70, the writer refers to "all the elementary teaching about Christ" and mentions among them "instruction about baptisms and laying on of hands."[22] Some, including Pope Paul VI, see in this reference "the origin of the Sacrament of Confirmation"[23] By the third century, this laying on of hands after Baptism had been coupled with an anointing, and by the fourth century the oil had become the sweet smelling mixture of oil with fragrances which the Greeks call 'myron', and we, in the West, call 'chrism'.

In the ancient world, the bishop celebrated the sacraments of Christian Initiation. In later ages, in the West, baptism (of infants especially) was carried out by priests, and so Confirmation became separated as villages awaited a visit from the bishop. This did not happen in the East. To this day, infant baptism is always followed by confirmation. St. Cyprian, the 3rd century bishop of Carthage in North Africa, spoke about Baptism and Confirmation as a "double sacrament".

## POOR EXPERIENCE AND POOR CATECHESIS

The Sacraments are outward signs of inward grace. How they are celebrated is supposed to express what is believed to be happening by God's grace. In short, the way we experience them is our enduring teacher of what they mean to us. Reflect on your own experience of Confirmation, in order to overcome any obstacles to your perception of what this essential element in your Christian Initiation signified and gave you.

Take as an example the way Catholics experienced Mass for many centuries. One man, alone, faced the wall, far away, quietly doing whatever he was doing, a server saying the responses. Meanwhile a church full of people got on with their own prayers, the choir did whatever singing took place and, above all, few if any of the congregation received Holy Communion. This went on until well into the 20th century. It took a mighty leap of the imagination, or a very enlightened faith, to think that whatever was happening at the altar was anything to do with the congregation. During my own childhood and adolescence whatever I understood about the Mass, I learned not by attending it, but by applying to my experience what I learned in the classroom; the same went for my confirmation.

My memory of being confirmed in 1946 or 47 is of being one of a crowd of class-mates, herded to and kneeling at the altar rails while somebody I had never seen before walked along dabbing our foreheads from a small pot and tapping us on the cheek. That this event took place when I was seven or eight years old was nothing to do with me or, for that matter, my parents. Confirmation took place when the bishop made his three-yearly canonical visitation of the parish. I had to be 'done' with all those who hadn't been done since his last visit. As to the prior catechesis, given at school, my teachers' explanation of what it was all about seemed very airy fairy and they had lost me completely by the time they got to the twelve fruits of the Holy Ghost. As a pre-pubescent child I just gave up on 'benignity, longanimity, continency and chastity'. I dare say they use other words nowadays. I had no idea why I was being confirmed - except that one had to be.

Perhaps this last point expresses far more than a child's bewilderment. Maybe it says something of those who had to prepare children for Confirmation. The plain fact is that the Sacrament of Confirmation is about the grace of mission and the Church had lost, to very large extent, any consciousness that lay people had anything to do with the Church's mission.

The great give away which revealed this attitude was the expression that a baptised, confirmed person thinking of offering himself for priestly ordination was said to be 'going into the Church'. Because lay people were not seen as having a role in the life of the Church, they needed no sacramental empowerment for it. Having forgotten why Confirmation exists, new reasons for its having to take place were invented.

It 'strengthened' you; it was the moment when you 'confirmed' your baptism. None of these rang true for me even as a boy. Nearly seventy years later, I remain a Roman Catholic, not because I think the Church always has a profound appreciation of all the gifts of the Spirit. It doesn't. My faith is not in the Church's fidelity but the Lord's. He is faithful and is totally committed to the Church he died for. I say this because I believe that the grace of Confirmation could be described in precisely those terms: it gives us the grace of faithfulness to the Lord Jesus as his witnesses, even to the point of losing everything.

The words with which we are anointed are, "Be sealed with the gift of the Holy Spirit." It is these words we should focus on.

Baptism and Confirmation change us *radically* but we have to accept and want the change to happen. Baptised in infancy and confirmed in childhood, we could not accept or refuse the gift by deliberate choice. Initiated as adults we are not permitted to approach the sacraments without this deliberated choice. However, as adults who were baptised in infancy and confirmed in childhood, we can and must make a new choice of all that Christian Initiation means.

## BORN WITH A MISSION

I have no desire to draw too strong a parallel between the birth of Jesus and his appearance in history with our own baptism and confirmation, but reflecting on what we believe happened to him may shed light on what has happened to us.

The infancy narratives exist to make one thing clear: Jesus did not become the Son of God in his resurrection and exaltation. On the contrary, the eternal Son of God became a man; as the Creed puts it: "He was conceived by the power of the Holy Spirit and born of the Virgin Mary." Nevertheless, this fact was not what one might call the "trigger" that set him on the life work that brought him to the Cross and Resurrection. His life took a completely new turn as a result of listening to the preaching of God's prophet, John, and submitting to John's baptism. In this event, the true status of this man standing among sinners was "confirmed" by the witness of heaven. Upon him, who had been conceived by the power of the Holy Spirit, the Spirit descended. Jesus did not become what he was not already, but this new anointing inspired and invigorated him to accomplish all that he was sent into the world to do. It was in the power of this anointing that he faced sin, and accepted his role as "the lamb of God who takes away the sins of the world." The Stanbrook Hymnal beautifully describes this:

> *"When Jesus comes to be baptized,*
> *He leaves the hidden years behind,*
> *The years of safety and of peace,*
> *To bear the sins of all mankind.*
>
> *The Spirit of the Lord comes down,*
> *Anoints the Christ to suffering,*
> *To preach the word, to free the bound*
> *And to the mourner comfort bring."* [24]

After his baptism, when Jesus appeared back in his home town, he announced himself as the person described in the prophet Isaiah, "The Spirit of the Lord God is upon me for he has anointed me; he has sent me to bring glad tidings…"[25]

In our baptism we were created anew by an outpouring of the Holy Spirit, adopted as sons and daughters of God. Indeed, it is this new birth granted us that we celebrate in the Christmas Liturgy. As ever, St. Leo expounds for us the Catholic faith our liturgy celebrates: "As we adore the birth of our Saviour we find that we are celebrating our own beginnings. For the birth of Christ is the origin of the people of Christ and the birthday of the Head is the birthday of the Body."[26] "Sharers now in the birth of Christ let us break with the deeds of the flesh. O Christian, be aware of your nobility – it is god's own nature that you share. Think of the Head, think of the Body of which you are a member."[27] In baptism we are indeed, "born of water and the Spirit." However, if we are to share not only Christ's life but his mission, we need the anointing that was given Jesus. The fourth Gospel speaks of Jesus breathing his Spirit into those he sends, "as I was sent by the Father." For St. Luke, with a different theological outlook, this outpouring occurs at Pentecost. Pope Paul VI, authorising the reformed rite after Vatican II said, the sacrament of Confirmation "In a certain way perpetuates the grace of Pentecost in the Church".[28]

Just as Jesus invoked the prophet Isaiah to testify to his home town what was happening among them, so Peter on the day of Pentecost invoked the prophets "I will pour out my spirit on all mankind. Your sons and daughters shall prophesy, your old men shall dream dreams, your young men see visions.[29] "These men are not drunk as you suppose… No. This is what the prophet spoke of."[30] It is the grace of Pentecost we receive in Confirmation.

## SHARING THE LIFE AND SHARING THE MISSION

Pope Paul's tentative phrase, 'in a certain way' belongs to the age in which it was written. Vatican II had recently reaffirmed the role of the baptised and confirmed obscured by centuries of clericalism. This mentality had implied that only the ordained could be evangelists: only the twelve apostles had been 'sent' with any real mandate to proclaim the Gospel. This tradition confused two issues. One is the apostolic authority to discern what is and what is not of the Gospel, a duty we see as belonging to bishops. The other is the responsibility of bearing witness to Jesus Christ, and sharing with all the gifts given us, which is the responsibility of all the baptised and confirmed – including the clergy! The role of bishops in regard to the mission of all indicates why Confirmation was reserved to them: all mission must be undertaken in communion with the bishop's apostolic leadership.

If we see in Jesus, even from the moment of his conception, mankind restored to the image and likeness of God, we may see in his birth the promise of what was to be given us in Baptism. As St. Augustine said, "The Spirit through whom men are reborn is the same Spirit through whom Christ was born."[31] If we see in Jesus at his baptism a man empowered to complete his life's work we may see in our having being confirmed our empowerment for our life's work. The error that a lot of us have to overcome in our personal theology, that is to say, in our perception of what it means to be a Christian, is that it is possible to be a member of the Body of Christ without any sharing in his mission. R.C.I.A. deems that adults who are not ready for Confirmation are not yet ready for Baptism. The Constitution on the Liturgy of the Second Vatican Council says, "by the sacrament of confirmation, (the baptised) are more perfectly bound to the Church and are enriched with a special strength of the Holy Spirit. Hence they are, as true witnesses of Christ, more strictly obliged to spread and defend the faith by word and deed."[32] Renewing our Baptismal Promises we renew both our call to share the life of Christ, and our being sent to share the Gospel with others. If we embrace the invitation to do this, we may be sure that the Lord will renew in us all the gifts we need for both these aspects of our Christian lives.

## MARKED FOR LIFE

According, then, to the words that complete our Baptism/Confirmation experience of Christian Initiation, we are 'sealed'. St. John speaks of Jesus as having been sealed, "on him the Father, God himself, has set his seal."[33] "You too," says St. Paul, "were sealed with the promised holy Spirit."[34] and he asks us to watch our conduct lest we grieve "the holy Spirit of God with which you were sealed."[35] We are to live our lives as Christians and confidently bear witness to him for "the one who gives us security with you in Christ and anointed us is God; he has also put his seal upon us and given us the Spirit in our hearts as a first instalment."[36]

We live in an age where people have no fear of 'making a statement,' as we say, by the designer labels they are proud to display on their clothes and even by what they do to their bodies by their piercings and tattoos. The more we become impressed *(that's an interesting Freudian slip)* by the reality of the seal by which we are marked, the more its reality will be manifested in the lifestyle we reveal to the world about us.

If we make our own this present programme of purification and enlightenment leading to a truly new commitment to the Lord Jesus at Easter, we shall know the Spirit's gift of joy. This joy is an effect of being anointed with 'the oil of gladness'. It comes from the Spirit–inspired conviction that we are indeed, called, chosen and sealed for life, bearing God's pledge of eternal life. Renewed in the Promised Gift we can make a new start in our discipleship and apostleship. We ourselves will benefit from the change and God alone knows what it can mean for the future of the Church he has called us into and equips us to serve.

# HOLY EUCHARIST

Our journey of faith began when, one way or another, we took heed of the words of the Lord Jesus, "Turn about, and believe the good news!" The experience of this starting point will have been different for each of us. Maybe it happened after years of avoiding God. Perhaps it occurred after years of searching for him. It might well have happened in our childhood. Attentive to other people of faith, we may have already accepted in our childish way that being attentive to God involved not having our own way all the time. At whatever point in our lives and whatever the circumstances, we did start to let God into our lives. In doing so, it has changed us. Changing in response to God's word continues throughout our lives. This is why Lent, just as it should be for those on the verge of Christian Initiation, can be a time of heart-felt change for all of us baptised, confirmed and admitted to Holy Communion these many years.

The New Testament scriptures use the Greek word metanoia when speaking of the radical change of heart the Gospel of Jesus Christ calls us to. These reflections on how one may prepare to renew our Baptismal Promises are rooted in the fact that the on-going process of metanoia, or conversion, takes us into ever deeper recesses of the heart. Were we ever foolish enough to convince ourselves that our conversion was complete, we would not stand still on the journey of faith; we would inevitably fall back.

I have no doubt that there is a period in our discipleship when we look around in our minds for something to confess. Children dragooned into too frequent confession once upon a time did it. I am told they even invented things to say. I recall my seminary days, when weekly confession was the practice, and such was the simplicity of our lives it was sometimes difficult to dig up anything worth confessing. However, this was more a question of spiritual immaturity than Christian perfection. One was simply not yet aware of the deep roots of selfishness, and our deep attachment to them that lie behind daily peccadilloes. As we mature in the way of faith, we may find that we can readily make our own the Church's prayer for the Elect made in the three Lenten Scrutinies. We have reached a significant moment in our discipleship when we ask the Lord to enlighten us about the healings we need which as yet are hidden from us. It is a very great grace to let the Holy Spirit expose to our consciousness deeper and deeper aspects of our human being where God has yet to reign.

The Spirit-inspired heart searching that leads to an ever deeper turning to the Lord, will enable us to appreciate more and more the holy treasures that we have so long shared in our experience of the Christian life. For the Elect these treasures are symbolised in the handing over of the Symbol of Faith and the Lord's Prayer. As we grow in our appreciation of the honour granted us by the Lord, we become aware of the communion of faith, prayer and life, granted us not only with fellow believers throughout the world today, but with the whole company now gathered to the Lord. This process of Lenten Purification and Enlightenment achieves its goal when renewing our Baptismal Promises we approach the Easter Sacraments themselves ready, willing and able to receive that renewal of Life in the Risen Christ they offer.

As a way of opening our minds and hearts to Lent's purification and enlightenment, we pondered what it is that God calls us from and what he calls us to. We said that whatever the mystery of sin may be, we all know that it is about 'ME, ME, ME'. We know instinctively, as we might say, such self-centredness is not the way to godliness. Indeed, it is the opposite. The Good News of Jesus Christ calls us to a way of life that is a radical undoing of sin's effects. God has called us to a life of love. St. John, speaking of this mystery said, "In this is love: not that we have loved God, but that he loved us and sent his Son as expiation for our sins."[37] On the night before he died, Jesus gave his disciples two commandments concerning our being called to live in this love, and our being sent to others as witnesses of this love. In the first, "Do this in memory of me,"[38] he gave them the memorial of his readiness to lay down his life for them. In the second he showed how his holy name would be honoured or disgraced by those who share in the Eucharist: "I give you a new commandment: love one another. As I have loved you, so you also should love one another. This is how all will know that you are my disciples, if you have love for one another."[39]

We have then, two commands and the measure of our obedience to one, must be the measure of our obedience to the other. We celebrate the Eucharist so that we may grow in the divine love for us that it celebrates, and, yielding to being so loved, we are given the power to love one another, creating in this world a sign of God's powerful love. St. John, as we all know, does not describe the giving of the Eucharist. Instead he describes an act of humble service Jesus carried out and which, if we do not allow him to perform for us, we can have no part in him. "Before the feast of Passover, Jesus knew that his hour had come to pass from of this world to the Father. He loved his own in the world and he loved them to the end."[40] The sign of this enduring love was to wash their feet.

In the person of Jesus, the Living One, has humbled himself before us who have sinned against him. Lent's purification and enlightenment is intended to create in us a humble and contrite heart. Having nothing to bring to the one who calls us, but our needs, we may approach the Sacraments of Initiation, or the remembrance of them once received, with full confidence. The Lord passes his judgement of forgiveness on all our sins, heals our selfishness, and actually pours out in our hearts the Holy Spirit. In the power of this promised Gift, we are enabled to love one another as Christ has loved us, creating from this love, a community that is fitted to bear witness to Jesus Christ. The Eucharistic Assembly in which the newly baptised and confirmed now take their place, is the most perfect manifestation of the Mystery of Faith into which they and we have been called.

The journey in faith began with our being called out of darkness and it brought us to the Holy Eucharist. It brings us to the heart of all creation. We made our way to this point by listening to the Gospel and embracing the religious heritage of the visible community of faith. Sharing its faith, we made a personal, life-long commitment to Jesus in our Baptismal Promises. We were plunged into the waters of new birth, anointed for mission with Chrism and led into the Christian Assembly, as sharers in the Sacrifice of Jesus Christ. St. Augustine says, "Every sacrifice is any work undertaken that we may adhere to God in a holy fellowship."[41] By making Christ's gift of the Eucharist our own, we are made sharers in the event by which God and mankind are eternally reconciled. We share in the new and everlasting covenant. In the power of the Spirit, we offer ourselves to the Father with Jesus, the Father accepts us in Christ and, in the power of the Spirit, we become 'one body, one spirit in Christ'.

It was said about our baptism that we did not physically go down into the tomb with the crucified Jesus; we did so only symbolically. Nevertheless, we were granted in that sign a true participation in all that Christ's dying and rising wrought for mankind. In a similar manner, by sharing in the sign which Jesus gave his disciples on the night before he died, saying, "Do this in memory of me" we are united with the Lord Jesus in his offering of himself to the Father, and with him we are accepted by the Father, nourished in the Divine Life and sent out in the power of the Spirit as Jesus was sent by the Father, as the bearers of this Good News.

## IN MEMORY OF ME

The modern English language we employ to speak about what Jesus actually said and did in giving us the Eucharist, falls far short of what the words are meant to indicate. In our everyday language, 'to remember' can mean nothing more than making a mental nod in the direction of something over and done with. We can of course remember something or some people with gestures of the utmost respect as happens at the Cenotaph on Remembrance Day. We can go further, as people do when remembering the anniversary of their marriage, they pledge their vows anew. In this sense something of the past is recalled in order to celebrate our present dedication to its continuing existence. When the people of the Old Covenant "remembered the mighty works of the Lord", they were actually celebrating their sharing in the blessings of which these works made them heirs. When they celebrated the Passover meal, they 'remembered' the event which brought them out of bondage and the covenant made at Mount Sinai. They 'called to mind' an event of the past by celebrating an action in the present, an action prescribed by God, and which celebrated the present generation's share in the covenant.

All this is the background to the words and actions of Jesus, when he gave his disciples the supper to be celebrated as his memorial, a sharing in the "blood of the new and everlasting covenant." Each of the four Eucharistic Prayers proclaims the faith of the Church in this matter. Each is worthy of our profoundest contemplation:

*"Father, we celebrate the memory of Christ, your Son. We, your people and your ministers, recall his passion, his resurrection from the dead and his ascension into glory;"*

*"In memory of his death and resurrection, we offer you, Father, this life-giving bread, this saving cup. We thank you for counting us worthy to stand in your presence and serve you."*

*"Father, calling to mind the death your son endured for our salvation, his glorious resurrection and ascension into heaven, and ready to greet him when he comes again, we offer you in thanksgiving this holy and living sacrifice."*

*"We recall Christ's death, his descent among the dead, his resurrection and his ascension to your right hand; and looking forward to his coming in glory, we offer you his body and blood the acceptable sacrifice which brings salvation to the whole world."*

The Eucharistic Prayers go on to describe the effect on those who make this remembrance:

*"May all of us who share in the body and blood of Christ be brought together in unity by the Holy Spirit."*

*"Look with favour on your Church's offering and see the Victim whose death has reconciled us to yourself. Grant that we, who are nourished by his body and blood, may be filled with his Holy Spirit, and become one body, one spirit in Christ."*

*"Lord, look upon this sacrifice which you have given to your Church; and by your Holy Spirit, gather all who share this one bread and one cup into the one body of Christ, a living sacrifice of praise."*

In this action and these words, the mighty work of God is remembered. That it may be abundantly clear that this 'remembrance' itself is a mighty work of God and not merely the action of man, the prayers invoke the Holy Spirit of God. Thus the Church bears witness to its faith that here in our midst the Almighty and Eternal God himself is accomplishing his work of grace.

*"Let your Spirit come upon these gifts to make them holy, so that they may become for us the body and blood of our Lord, Jesus Christ."*

*"And so, Father, we bring you these gifts. We ask you to make them holy by the power of your Spirit, that they may become the body and blood of your Son, our Lord Jesus Christ, at whose command we celebrate this eucharist."*

*"Father, may this Holy Spirit sanctify these offerings. Let them become the body and blood of Jesus Christ our Lord as we celebrate the great mystery which he left us as an everlasting covenant."*

In these profound words, we can see why the Holy Eucharist has been described as the 'source and summit' of all the Church's activities. All evangelisation, all catechesis, indeed, the whole process of Christian formation leads to our sharing in the Eucharist. This is the centre point of the entire Mystery of Faith and it is summed up in the doxology and great amen:

*"Through him, with him and in him, in the unity of the Holy Spirit, all honour and glory is yours, Almighty Father, for ever and ever. Amen"*[42]

At the Easter Vigil, we shall renew our baptismal promises and recall with thanksgiving our baptism and confirmation. Believing all that God in Christ has brought about through these sacred signs, we may take our place among the priestly people, Head and members, worshipping the Father in spirit and in truth. On that occasion, attend the Holy Eucharist as would the newly baptised, remembering that this would have been the first time that they had been admitted beyond the threshold of the Temple.

Hear as if for the first time. See the actions as though never before. Hear the Risen Lord Jesus invite you, "Take and eat;" "Take and drink." As you respond with the words, "Lord, I am not worthy" do so in a full remembrance of the sacramental initiation, the cleansing and the anointing by which the Lord brings you into the Holy of Holies. If we have embraced the purification and enlightenment Lent offers, we shall have embraced our unworthiness and in doing so, been able to offer the Lord a humble and contrite heart, open to the Gift by which we are made worthy to stand in the Lord's presence and serve him. Renewed thus in the very foundational grace of all Christian living, we may go from the Easter Mass, newly restored witnesses of all that we have been called to believe.

## PERSONAL AND CORPORATE RENEWAL

It can do only good if individual believers, reading this book, awaken to the grace of renewal offered in the Easter Liturgy. However, this grace will blossom into something more wonderful and bear abundant fruit only when we realise that no Christian exists in isolation. God offers renewal not simply to individuals, but principally to the community of faith he has brought into existence and to which he has entrusted a mission. To take our place in this community clearly involves us in personal decision making. But the decision is to join with others in the faith they professed before we did. It is only through the witness of the community that we came to a knowledge of Jesus. It is only through the ministry of the community that we came to faith in him, and it is only by participating in their worship that we become members of Christ sharing his life and mission.

The community of faith and the Liturgy it celebrates are not like background music to our personal pieties. On the contrary, the Liturgy celebrates our sharing in something of which we are not the authors. This corporate sense is an essential feature of authentic Catholicism. In recent centuries it has become blunted by an individualistic attitude to salvation. Deprived of any real sense of sharing in the Church's mission in the world, lay people could not be blamed for imagining that the only point of the sacraments was to help them 'save their souls'. During the twentieth century powerful movements of the Spirit drew the Church out of this mentality, and one of the most important ways of refocusing the Church was Liturgical renewal.

The Second Vatican Council espoused a root and branch reform of the Sacred Liturgy. One of its principal aims in doing so was to rekindle an awareness in the assembly, the gathering of the scattered children of God, that it is brought into being by the Paschal Mystery of Christ's death and exaltation. Its entire life and worship springs from this central reality. To that end, the Council authorised a total revision of the way we celebrate the Liturgy. The task of refocusing the Church's mind on the central mystery involved reforming the Liturgical Calendar, and Pope Paul VI published it in 1969.[43] It is interesting to notice that in doing so he used the word 'restore' three times in one paragraph in connection with the actions of his predecessors in the decades before the Council.

He wrote about St. Pius X and Blessed John XXIII taking action that "Sunday might be *restored* to its former dignity" as "the original feast day." "They also *restored* the season of Lent to its rightful place." And Pope Pius XII "decreed that the night of the passover be *restored* to its proper place as a vigil." His entire argument assumes that something had got out of kilter; something had been side-lined or was being ignored in our worship. All the work of *restoration* led to a renewal of the way we celebrate the event about which this book has been written: the Easter Vigil. The 'mother of all vigils' was restored to its central place in the life of the Church because, "at this rite the sacraments of Christian Initiation are celebrated, and the People of God *reaffirms its spiritual covenant with the Risen Lord.*" This wonderful expression reveals the deepest meaning of the restored Easter Triduum.

Once we have grasped this truth we shall understand why the fifty days of Easter were called 'the Great Sunday'. We shall see why it is said, "What Sunday is to the week, the solemnity of Easter is to the liturgical year." We shall see why in a tradition that comes from the Apostles themselves, the day on which the Lord rose again came to be called 'the Lord's day', and the great assembly was held not only to read in the Scripture those things which are about him, but to celebrate the great sign he gave us, recognising him in the breaking of bread.

God's Church and every member of it are unceasingly called by God, always being called to faith and a renewal of his saving grace. We celebrate this fact every Sunday, but once a year we celebrate the same fact most solemnly. We renew our commitment, and are nourished in our faith and service whenever we share in the Sacred Liturgy, but at Easter, focusing so directly as it does on the foundational event which brought the Church into being, the whole People of God renews its commitment to the Covenant.

This book has been written that individual believers may consider how important a grace is being offered us in the invitation to renew our baptismal promises. However, as has been pointed out, no Christian believer exists in isolation or is entrusted with the mission in isolation. Of its nature, Christian Initiation *incorporates* us into the Mystery of Faith, the Risen Christ, Head and members, active in the world in completion of the mission entrusted to the Lord Jesus by the Father. While an appeal is being made to *each* believer to embrace the grace of renewal offered in the Liturgy of Lent and Easter, it is made to them as members of the one, holy, catholic and apostolic assembly, called and sent. Easter celebrates not the individual promises of individual believers, but the vocation and empowerment of the whole assembly: the renewal of the covenant. Easter is renewal of a shared calling and empowerment. A local church which enters into the true meaning of Easter will be renewed not only in its individual members but in its shared life and mission. It is greatly to be desired that individuals make a new commitment to the covenant, but what might one expect were a whole parish community to do so!

What flowering of grace may we expect for any parish community which awakens to the fact that in its Liturgy it is being invited by the Lord, precisely as the people called to be his own, to renew its pledge to him? This is the spouse born from the Lord's side as he slept the sleep of death on the cross. This is the faithful spouse who will be adorned with all the gifts of the Spirit needed to share Christ's life and mission. This is the company of believers who will embody a powerful manifestation of the Spirit in all His gifts and ministries bringing to the world a new evangelisation.

## CHAPTER SEVEN

# A CHURCH WITH A SENSE OF MISSION

Forty years ago, I asked myself if I knew of any parish in my local church that was ready to take up the work of evangelisation, catechesis and liturgical formation described in the Rite of Christian Initiation of Adults. Praise God, many parish structures and many attitudes have changed since then. However, we have to ask ourselves if the pastoral structures, pastoral priorities, and the mindset we have inherited can sustain the task in hand.

How do our parishes see themselves in relation to the world in which they exist? Do they see themselves as existing to bring faith in Jesus Christ to people who scarcely know his name? Do they see themselves as beacons of hope in the midst of people who live without faith of any kind? Do they see themselves as existing to be recognised as a 'sacrament of reconciliation between God and mankind and among men'?[1] We have to know where we come from if we are to work out the way to where we should be. Why were today's Roman Catholic parishes in England and Wales set up? How ready are they today to become instruments of a new evangelisation?

## WHERE WE COME FROM

The modern Roman Catholic Church in England and Wales came into existence just over one hundred and sixty years ago, when Pope Pius IX created a Hierarchy of England and Wales in 1850. In the preceding decades, civil law, canon law and a rapid growth in numbers had all contributed to making the Roman Catholic community in this country something it had not been for centuries. Despite generations of anti-Catholic legislation, small groups had managed to cling on to the practice of their religion so that by the beginning of the 19th century Catholics in England and Wales saw themselves as a despised remnant on the fringes of society. Blessed John Henry Newman in his 'Second Spring' sermon of 1852 conjures, perhaps from his childhood, a deeply moving picture of its marginal existence. He speaks of, "an old-fashioned house of gloomy appearance, closed in with high walls, with an iron gate, and yews, and the report attaching to it that 'Roman Catholics' lived there; but who they were, or what they did, or what was meant by calling them Roman Catholics, no one could tell; though it had an unpleasant sound, and told of form and superstition."[2]

However, their numbers began to mushroom. This rapid expansion began with immigration from Europe as a result of the French Revolution and then, notably, from Ireland. In 1829 Parliament passed the Roman Catholic Relief Act, the culmination of a growing movement for Roman Catholic Emancipation. In 1850 Pope Pius IX created the modern hierarchy. However, neither of these events enabled Roman

Catholics to see themselves, or their institutions as integrated into society. On the contrary they appear to have reinforced a victim mentality.

Newman spoke about the Relief Acts as springing not from any respect or admiration for the Roman Catholic Church. On the contrary, he saw the changes in legislation as the effect of an attitude towards a section of the population regarded as "so utterly contemptible, that contempt gave birth to pity... under the notion that their opinions were simply too absurd ever to spread."[3] When Pope Pius IX appointed a hierarchy, his action was regarded as 'papal aggression' and created a public outrage of monstrous proportions.[4] Perhaps this act was seen as the act of a dog biting the hand that had generously thrown it some substantial scraps.

The heirs of the old recusant families carried the weight of centuries of political and social exclusion by reason of the penal laws; the 'poor Irish' immigrants were excluded by reason of their poverty and their Irishness. Despite the fact that the Roman Catholic Church had been granted legal existence, it saw itself surrounded by enemies and although its numbers grew and grew during the next hundred years, something of this excluded, marginalised mentality endured right up to the eve of the Second Vatican Council. (1962-65)

What could be the achievement of a church which, sometimes for good reasons, saw itself in this way? Was it to convert the populace to the Gospel of Christ? No. It existed in what was presumed by all to be an already Christian country. Its main focus was to establish the visible and authoritative presence in British society of Roman Catholic institutions. What is more, this task was not seen as introducing something new in British society. It was spoken of and offered to society as the restoration of something lost.

If it had any missionary outreach it was to convert Protestants back to Roman Catholicism, not unbelievers to the Gospel of Christ. It is fair to say that the main thrust of the Roman Catholic Church's efforts in the United Kingdom, between the 'restoration' of the Hierarchy in 1850 and the opening of the Second Vatican Council in 1962, was that Protestants should recognise the institutions of the Roman Catholic Church as the authentic expression of apostolic authority. This is undoubtedly one aspect of Catholic Christianity but it can scarcely be described as evangelisation.

Those people who actually sought to join the Roman Catholic Church, far from being welcomed as fellow believers seeking full communion, were called 'converts'. This word is used to describe unbelievers who are converted to Christian faith. Nowadays, the R.C.I.A. makes a sharp distinction between them and Christians of another Church, or ecclesial community, who wish to come into full communion with the Catholic Church.[5] The welcome given 'converts' was an absolution from heresy, schism and the canonical penalties incurred thereby. The tone of the ceremony was scarcely the welcome home of a brother or sister; it was rather the juridical reconciliation of someone ready to abjure error. Converts 'submitted' to the authority of the Church. Even the most superficial acquaintance with the ritual of reconciling converts reveals this attitude. As I recall it, the priest, wearing a purple stole, sat on the sanctuary side of the altar rails; the convert knelt there and, having abjured his errors, received absolution and the lifting of canonical sanctions.

This was the historical situation in which today's parishes were created, the mindset which gave them birth. They simply were not set up to be centres of evangelisation and certainly not of a "new evangelisation." Pastoral techniques simply did not take into account the task of leading unbelievers outside the Church to faith in Jesus Christ. Pastoral practice was based on the idea that people are born into Catholic families, went to Catholic schools, met other Catholics in parish youth clubs, married them and sent their children to Catholic schools. That was the system. Outreach to persons not born into Catholic families was not perceived as a task for the parish itself, or for individual parishioners. People who married into Catholic families were given some introduction that it was hoped would get them to become Catholics, but there was no parish-based policy of reaching out to the 'non-Catholic' population. 'Converts' were people who made the first move. Until relatively recent times, the mind-set of the Roman Catholic Church in England and Wales was inward looking and defensive.

It has to be remembered that given the historical situation, that is to say, the assumption that the Roman Catholic Church was being re-introduced into an already Christianised society, any systematic approach to people of other denominations would have been regarded as proselytising rather than evangelising.

## WHERE WE ARE

If the Roman Catholic Church of the twenty-first century is ever to flourish here, it must ask serious questions about its inherited sense of priorities. It has to awaken to the needs of spiritually starved multitudes to whom the Lord Jesus Christ is sending the dwindling band of Christians of England and Wales. The Church has to ask itself once more, "Why do we exist here?" The answer is not the same as it was in 1850 and the century that followed, for the religious landscape is utterly changed.

The Mass-going population in the United Kingdom may well be the largest group of Christians who worship regularly. Nevertheless, the Roman Catholic Church is a shrinking church. In my own part of the world where Non-conformist chapels once thrived, congregations have evaporated, and buildings have become carpet warehouses or small factories. Anglican congregations are a fraction of what they once were. Poor preaching encouraged Roman Catholics to imagine that this could not happen to them. Yet, in the city where I live, Mass attendance which in 1951 represented 6% of the total population has fallen over sixty years to 2.1 %.

Sociologists may show us many reasons for the decline. Among them we may gladly acknowledge the lack of social pressure to conform to any form of Christian observance in a more secular and affluent society than that of earlier decades. We also know that there are any number of factors in our society that undermine both Christian faith and morality. Catholic sources are forever denouncing them. However, if the decline in Mass attendance actually represents a corrosion of faith, where does the corrosion begin? Is it not from factors within the Church rather than from outside influences? If people have fallen away from the practice of the Roman Catholic religion, at least to the extent of never or rarely attending Mass, if people have 'lapsed', from what have they lapsed? Do these considerations not bring us back to the charge that within our pastoral system many people have been 'sacramentalised' without having been 'evangelised'? I am not persuaded that people who have been exposed to the beauty and the challenge of the Gospel of Christ easily and readily repudiate it.

Great numbers of people get no nearer the Gospel than the witness of half-baked commitment, sometimes a total lack of commitment, on the part of those who brought them to the sacraments in their infancy and childhood. For others, their experience of sacramental worship, while it may be a severe test for their patience and attention, never stimulates them to reverence and awe in the mystery this worship is supposed to express. Some, feeling robbed of the forms of worship and devotion they knew as children, have gone away. Some people, judging leaders of the world-wide church to be unfaithful to the grace of reform and renewal proclaimed in the Second Vatican

Council, fall away because of disappointment. Others, hitherto faithful in their religious practice, are disgusted by corrupt practices and hypocrisy in the church and can stomach it no longer. Their experience of the Church is a stumbling block. It may not be an obstacle to faith in the Gospel of Christ but it is surely an obstacle to faith in a church which claims to profess the Gospel.

## WHERE ARE WE GOING?

In the face of these and many other considerations, what must be the response of those who choose to remain? It is the vocation of our generation of believers, so I believe, to imitate Christ's own faithfulness, and the faithfulness of those whose heirs the leaders of the Roman Catholic Church in 1850 claimed to be.

We have to bring to a Church in sore need of evangelical reform and renewal, that faithfulness we believe Jesus Christ has for his beloved spouse. We have to be renewed in a love not for the human traditions and forms that we love about 'our' church. All who wish to keep faith with the visible, hierarchic, sacramental Church must be explicit in their profession of faith. I mean faith in the Living Lord Jesus who is wedded to this visible, concrete expression of his presence in the world. In my own experience, at a time of deepest gloom in my local church, it seemed that the Lord was saying, "You have problems with this Church? I died for it." We must have the courage to say that we have no human reason whatsoever for belonging to the

Roman Catholic Church, but we are staying. We have been given Christ's gift of faith in him and in his fidelity to his Church. That is all. It is the name of this Christ that we proclaim and to this Church we invite people.

We have models of such fidelity; the very men and women who died as criminals but whom the 'restored' Catholic Church of 1850 passionately claimed as its own. We may claim to be the heirs of the martyrs of the sixteenth and seventeenth centuries if we too keep faith with a Church in sore need of evangelical reform and renewal.

Many of the institutions of the Church in whose name, St. John Fisher and St. Thomas More went to the scaffold were, and had been for some time, a scandalous offence to the name of Jesus. The Papal office for which, in particular, they sacrificed their lives, was occupied, and had been occupied for some time by men of the most disgraceful reputation. Recognising these grave evils with eyes wide open, they laid down their lives for Jesus Christ by dying for the unity of his beloved Church. They did this in the conviction that it was for this very church he had laid down his life. If we would share the same faith of these great believers, we should look to the shortcomings we find in the Church of our own generation and, in many ways, praise God for the easy time we have. We should see it as the highest honour granted us in our Christian vocation to keep faith with the Lord Jesus, not so much in the face of the malice shown by his enemies, as bearing the shame brought on his holy name by the company of those known to the world as his followers. This faithfulness to the concrete reality penetrated by the Divine Presence is authentic, Catholic Christianity.

In 1535, the aged bishop John Fisher, in the last minutes of his life, being led to the scaffold on Tower Hill, turned to his New Testament for strength and made this prayer. "O Lord! this is the last time that ever I shall open this book; let some comfortable place now chance unto me, whereby I thy poor servant may glorify thee in this my last hour." For a man who faced death because he found it impossible to separate his fidelity to the Lord Jesus from his fidelity to the visible communion of Christ's Church, his prayer was answered thus, "Now this is eternal life, that they should know you, the only true God and the one whom you sent, Jesus Christ. I glorified you on earth by accomplishing the work that you gave me to do."[6] In worship of this most delicate grace, this sign that the Lord was stood by him in his confession, it is said of him, "With that he shut his book together and said, 'here is even learning enough for me to my life's end'."[7] May it be so for all who say they share his faith.

## FAITHFULNESS REVEALED IN SERVICE

If the number of Mass-goers is now smaller than for generations, we have to ask why those who still worship with the Church continue to do so. The answer may reveal to us the presence of a great grace in the Church. We shall discover among a great number of people who continue to take part regularly in the Church's worship, Christ's gift of faithful love. Despite whatever is wrong or deficient in the Church, we cannot fail to recognise the presence of this faithful love, for with this love, there is revealed a vibrant sign of life that bodes well for the future.

Whatever the fall-off in Mass attendance, we would be blind to the facts if we did not own with joy that nowadays, there are more Mass-goers actively engaged in the work of the Church than ever there was in the Church before the Second Vatican Council. They may not turn up in any numbers to take part in the private devotions that formed the greater part of parish life and worship in the heyday of 'restored' 19th. century Roman Catholicism, but there are actually more and more people willing to engage in the Church's mission. This continues to be the case even when lay-people find that their engagement in all that they were baptised and confirmed to do is hampered by clericalist attitudes, actions and, sometimes, systems. This is a triumph of grace. It is a sound basis on which today's Church can build for tomorrow.

To all who wish to dedicate themselves to the task which faces the Church, these reflections are offered. The Lord is faithful and will honour the desire of anyone who sets out to re-establish the foundations of our membership of the Church: our vocation and sacramental empowerment. The Lord has not abandoned his people but he does invite them to rediscover his real presence in the manifold signs of their having been called to and empowered for a life of faith and mission. In being re-evangelised we shall become an evangelising Church.

# NOTES

## Introduction: Why ask the Question

1. "Christians today have to rediscover the heart of the Christian message; they have been sufficiently `sacramentalised;' they have not been sufficiently `evangelized'." Cardinal Suenens. (The Tablet, 19th September 1992)
2. The importance of the charismatic gifts in the work of evangelisation, I have written about in *Called and Sent*, New Life Publishing, Luton, 2011
3. Vat.II 'Sacrosanctum Concilium' (art.10)
4. ibid., (art.106)
5. Rite of Christian Initiation of Adults (R.C.I.A.) no. 75
6. Apostolic Constitution, 'Divinae Consortium Naturae' Aug. 15, 1971)
7. Motu Proprio 'Ministeria Quaedam' August, 1972
8. The Roman Missal, ICEL trans. 1974, p.216
9. ibid.
10. Acts 4, 31 "As they prayed, the place where they were gathered shook, and they were all filled with the Holy Spirit and continued to speak the word of God with boldness."
11. Luke 11, 11-13

## Chapter 1 : A Sense of the Mystery

1. R.C.I.A. no.75
2. Rev.1, 18
3. John 20, 28
4. John 6, 44
5. John 20, 30
6. Catechism of the Catholic Church, para. 43
7. ibid. (cf. Summa Contra Gentiles, 1.30)
8. Leo the Great, Sermon 12, the Passion of the Lord, 3, 6
9. Colossians 3, 3

10. 1 Tim. 3, 16
11. 1 John 1, 1 (The Jerusalem Bible, Darton, Longman & Todd Ltd, London, 1966)
12. Catechism of the Catholic Church, para. 170
13. Heb. 6, 19
14. 'Lumen Gentium', art. 1
15. 'Lumen Gentium', art. 9, para. 3
16. J.D. Chrichton, 'The Church's Worship', Geoffrey Chapman, London, 1964
17. E. Schillebeeckx, O.P., Rowman & Littlefield. (1963)
18. St. Augustine, Tract on John, 6, chap.1. no.7
19. St. Leo, Sermon 2 on the Ascension of the Lord, 2
20. St. Augustine, Tract on John, 21, 8
21. Is. 6, 5
22. The Roman Missal, ICEL trans. 1974, p. 411

## Chapter 2 : Called and Chosen

1. 1 Sam. 2, 19
2. 1 Sam. 3, 6
3. Karl Rahner, 'The Trinity', trans. Joseph Donceel (Tunbridge Wells: Burns and Oates, 1970), 10-11.
4. Eph. 2, 14-15
5. 1 Pet. 2, 4-5
6. John 2, 19
7. 1 Cor. 3, 16
8. 1 Cor. 6, 19
9. R.C.I.A. no. 50
10. John 15, 16
11. http//biblecommenter.com/john/15-16.htm
12. Eph. 1, 4
13. I Cor. 2, 7
14. Col. 1, 27

## Chapter 3 : Purified

1. Rom. 7, 13-25
2. Phil. 3, 6
3. Mk. 2, 17
4. Luke 7, 47
5. 'Amazing Grace' John Newton (1725–1807),
6. Eucharistic Prayer no.1, The Roman Missal, ICEL trans. 1974, p. 496
7. John 8, 31
8. Joel 2, 13
9. Ezek. 36, 26
10. Heb. 4, 15
11. Matt. 26, 41
12. Mk. 1, 15
13. 1 John 1,8
14. R.C.I.A. nos.128-131
15. John 20, 31
16. Gen. 18, 15
17. Lk. 23, 34
18. Rom. 5, 20
19. Mk. 1, 40-42 (The Jerusalem Bible, Darton, Longman & Todd Ltd, London, 1966)
20. Lk. 1, 67-79 ('The Divine Office', Collins, London & Glasgow, 1974)
21. Gen. 18, 14
22. 'Exultet', Easter Vigil. The Roman Missal, ICEL trans. 1974, p.199.

## Chapter 4 : Enlightened

1. Ex. 3, 11
2. Ex. 2, 11-15
3. Ex. 17, 7
4. Gen. 28, 15
5. Jos. 1, 5
6. Judges 6, 15
7. 1 Sam. 3, 19

8. Jer. 1, 7
9. Mt. 1, 23. (cf. Is. 7, 14)
10. Mt. 28, 20
11. Heb. 6, 19
12. Col. 3, 3
13. Rom. 8, 39
14. John 10, 27-30
15. Dt. 30, 11-14
16. I John 4, 16
17. I Cor. 13
18. John 10, 10
19. John 10, 9
20. John Marriott, (1780-1825)
21. I John 3, 2-3
22. 'One Hand, One Heart', West Side Story, Sondheim/Bernstein, 1957
23. Ps. 8
24. Ps. 138/9, 13-15
25. St. Irenaeus, 'Against the Heresies', Bk.4, 20, 7.

## Chapter 5 : Entrusted with God's Gifts

1. R.C.I.A. no. 134
2. Lk. 16., 12
3. 'Faith of our Fathers', Frederick W. Faber, 1814-1863
4. 'Ecclesiam Suam', Encyclical Letter of Pope Paul VI, August 6th, 1964
5. Ps. 138/9, 1-6
6. Dt. 4, 35
7. R.C.I.A. no. 134
8. St. John Damascene, 'Orthodox Faith', 3.24
9. 1 Cor. 2, 16 (cf. Is. 40, 13)
10. Matt. 6, 9-13
11. Lk. 11, 2-14
12. St. Irenaeus, 'Against the Heresies', Bk. 5, Preface
13. St. Athanasius, 'The Incarnation of the Word', 54

14. John 14
15. John 11. 52
16. Mk. 14, 36
17. Rom. 8, 15
18. Gal. 4, 6
19. Lk. 15, 7
20. I Cor. 13, 12
21. Letters of St. Ignatius of Antioch: to the Romans, chap.6
22. John 4, 23
23. Proverbs 9, 10
24. I Cor. 1, 24
25. I Cor. 15, 24 & 28
26. Revelations 22, 20
27. Revelations 11, 17 ('The Divine Office', Collins, London & Glasgow, 1974)
28. I Tim. 2, 3
29. Acts 4, 32-35
30. Matt. 5, 48
31. James 1, 13-14
32. 1 Cor. 10, 13
33. Hebrews 4, 14-16
34. Col. 1, 13
35. I Thess. 5, 17
36. Rom. 8, 31-39
37. 'Ava: A Biography' by Roland Flamini Coward, McCann & Geoghegan, New York, 1983
38. 1 Sam. 16, 7
39. Jer. 17, 9
40. Ps. 51, 12
41. Ez. 11, 19-20
42. Eph. 3, 17
43. The Roman Missal, ICEL trans. 1974, p. 204
44. Isaiah 6, 8-10

45. Isaiah 53, 1
46. Isaiah 6, 9
47. Rev. 3, 14-12
48. Acts 2, 37-39
49. Rev. 15, 3-4
50. Ex. 15
51. Eph. 3, 14-21

## Chapter 6 : Christian Initiation
1. Mark 1, 11
2. St. Augustine, Commentary on Ps.60
3. 1 Cor. 11, 25
4. St. Leo, Sermon 51
5. St. Augustine, Tract. on John, 15, 10-17
6. John. 4, 10
7. John. 4, 14
8. John. 7, 38-39
9. John. 9, 7
10. St. Augustine, Tract on John, 34, 8-9
11. St. John Chrysostom, 'Homily on the Gospel of St. John' "And why did he not use water instead of spittle for the clay? He was about to send the man to Siloam: in order therefore that nothing might be ascribed to the fountain, but that you might learn that the same power proceeding from His mouth, both formed and opened the man's eyes, He 'spat on the ground'; this at least the Evangelist signified, when he said, 'And made clay of the spittle'. Then, that the successful issue might not seem to be of the earth, He told him to wash."
12. The Roman Missal, ICEL trans. 1974, p.203.
13. Rom. 6, 3-7
14. Jerusalem Catechesis, 21. Mystagogia 3, 1-3
15. I John 3, 2-3
16. John 11, 25
17. John 14, 6

18. Rom. 10, 8-9 (cf. Deut. 30, 14)
19. 'Prayer'[1] 'The English Poems of George Herbert'. p.70. J.M. Dent & Sons Ltd. 1974
20. The Roman Missal, ICEL trans. 1974, p.143.
21. Jerusalem Catechesis 21, Mystagogica 3. 1-3.
22. Heb. 6, 2
23. Apostolic Constitution, 'Divinae Consortium Naturae', Aug. 15, 1971
24. cf 'The Divine Office', vol. 1, p.371. Collins, London and Glasgow, 1974
25. Is. 61, 1
26. St. Leo the Great, Sermon 6, Nativity of the Lord
27. St. Leo the Great, Sermon 1, Nativity of the Lord
28. Apostolic Constitution, 'Divinae Consortium Naturae', Aug. 15, 1971
29. Joel 3, 1-2
30. Acts. 2, 15-17
31. St. Augustine, 'On the Predestination of the Saints', Chap.15
32. 'Lumen Gentium', art. 6
33. John 6. 27
34. Eph.1.13
35. Eph.4.30
36. 2 Cor.1, 22
37. 1 Jo. 4.10
38. Luke 22, 19
39. John 13, 34-35
40. John 13. 1
41. St. Augustine, 'The City of God', Bk. 10, 6
42. The Roman Missal, ICEL trans. 1974, p.485-507
43. The Roman Missal, ICEL trans. 1974, p lxxxi

# Chapter 7: A Church with a Sense of Mission
1. 'Lumen Gentium.' Art. 1

2. Jn. Henry Newman (1801-1890), A Sermon delivered to the First Provincial Council of Westminster, 1852. www.fordham.edu/halsall/mod/newman-secondspring.asp

3. ibid.

4. "One of the grossest acts of folly and impertinence which the Court of Rome has ventured to commit since the Crown and the people of England threw off its yoke." (The Times, 14 October, 1850) quoted in 'Protestant versus Catholic in Mid-Victorian England' Walter Arnstein, Columbia: University of Missouri Press, 1982.

5. "Those who have been baptized in another Church or ecclesial community should not be treated as catechumens or so designated." R.C.I.A., Appendix III Reception into Full Catholic Communion para. 30 p. 395

6. John, 17, 3-4

7. The Church History of Britain, vol.2; p.63. Thomas Fuller, Thomas Tegg, London, 1842.

*Further copies of this book can be obtained from*

**Goodnews Books**
*Upper level
St. John's Church Complex
296 Sundon Park Road
Luton, Beds. LU3 3AL*

*www.goodnewsbooks.net
orders@goodnewsbooks.net
01582 571011*